THE REVIEWERS RAVED ABOUT
How to Be a Canadian

· · · · ·

"A wry, funny look at Canadian sports, leisure, cuisine, history, driving habits and culture . . . Authors Will and Ian Ferguson pry a laugh out of nearly every aspect of Canadian life. One of the funniest books to cross my desk."
Victoria Times-Colonist

"A hilarious exploration of what it means to be Canadian."
Airlines Magazine

"It's a treat to nestle down for a giggle with *How to Be a Canadian*. It made me glad that I already am one."
Montreal Gazette

"The Ferguson brothers have a way of hitting it on the head so hard you don't know whether to laugh or cry."
January Magazine

"You want funny, Canadian funny? We're talking about the Brothers Ferguson."—*Edmonton Journal*

"The Fergusons, Will and Ian, have contributed much to the spicy energy of Canadian history, fiction and comedy."
Aritha van Herk

"It's a grand thing to be a Ferguson brother in this country. You're always winning Leacock Medals for Humour, and everything you write is expected to be a significant contribution to Canadiana, not to mention satire. It's all worked out beautifully so far . . . The country according to the brothers Ferguson."—*Vancouver Province*

Will Ferguson
& Ian Ferguson

HOW TO BE A
CANADIAN

Douglas & McIntyre

Douglas and McIntyre (2013) Ltd.
P.O. Box 219
Madeira Park, B.C., Canada, von 2h0
www.douglas-mcintyre.com

First published in 2001
First U.S. edition in 2003

Library and Archives Canada Cataloguing in Publication
Ferguson, Will
How to be a Canadian / Will Ferguson & Ian Ferguson. — New ed.
Originally published under title:
How to be a Canadian, even if you already are one

ISBN 978-1-55365-311-0

1. National characteristics, Canadian—Humor.
2. Canadian wit and humor (English) 1. Ferguson, Ian, 1959– 11. Title.
FC173.F458 2007   c818'.5402   C2007-903037-8

Editing by Barbara Pulling
Cover design by Naomi MacDougall and Jessica Sullivan
Text design by Peter Cocking and Jessica Sullivan
Cover illustration by Ryan Heshka

Printed and bound in Canada by Friesens
Printed on acid-free paper that is forest friendly (100% post-consumer
recycled paper) and has been processed chlorine free.
Distributed in the U.S. by Publishers Group West

We gratefully acknowledge the financial support of the Canada
Council for the Arts, the British Columbia Arts Council, the Province
of British Columbia through the Book Publishing Tax Credit,
and the Government of Canada through the Book Publishing Industry
Development Program (BPIDP) for our publishing activities.

CONTENTS

. . . .

*(In which Will shamelessly milks the name of one of
Canada's most respected authors for all it's worth)*

*S*o I'M AT THIS cocktail party, right?
And Margaret Atwood is there, and
she can't keep her hands off me. Everywhere I go, she's
clinging to me. And I'm like, "Whoa, lady, get a grip." All
night long, she's following me around, spilling her drink
and slurring her speech, saying, "Wait, wait. I have this
great idea for your next book." And I'm like, "What*ever*."

Okay, so that's not quite how it happened. I was in fact
the cling-er, not the cling-ee. It was at a bookstore opening
in Calgary, and Margaret Atwood was the guest of honour.
Not that I was intimidated or anything. No sir. With a few
drinks in me and a belly full of hubris, I latched myself
onto Her Royal Self and refused to leave until she acknowl-
edged my existence.

Margaret (or "Ms. Atwood" to those of you who are not
on an accosting basis with the First Lady of Canadian Letters) was very gracious. Yes, she had heard of *Why I Hate*

Canadians. No, she didn't think it sucked. Yes, she was working on another novel. No, she wouldn't tell me what it was about. No, not even a hint.

And then, just in passing, she said, in that wonderful low clipped voice of hers (the anecdote works a lot better if you do your own impression of Margaret Atwood as you read this): "Do you know what your next book should be? You should write a guidebook for newcomers. There was a book by a Hungarian writer, back in the 1950s, I believe. I think it was called 'How to Be an Englishman.' Very funny. You should do one about Canadians."

"Like lessons on how to be Canadian?"

"That's right. For example, talking about the weather. In Canada, you must always present it in the form of a question"—and here she did, I swear, a perfect imitation of a Canadian hoser—*"Hey there! Cold enough for ya?"*

"I see. But what if it's summer?"

She sighed. I was obviously a bit thick. "Well, then you say, *'Hot enough for ya?'* Or *'Wet enough for ya?'* And so on."

I thought her idea was splendid, and indeed, so great was my enthusiasm for the project, and so sweeping were my arm gestures, that I succeeded in spilling my drink all over myself. But not a drop on Ms. Atwood.

Later, I tracked down the book she was referring to, and, sure enough, a Hungarian writer by the name of George Mikes had written a guide to English customs called *How to Be an Alien.* It was published in 1946, and it provided a succinct overview of British society.

So why not write a handy guide for new Canadians as well, one explaining how best to fit in amongst the hearty and stalwart inhabitants of the Great White North? My entire book proposal consisted of two words: "Margaret Atwood." It was the easiest sales pitch I ever made.

So here's a handy tip for any aspiring young writers out there: When it comes time to pitch your book idea, don't forget those five little words, "As suggested by Margaret Atwood . . ." Boy oh boy, do publishers snap to attention when you say that. *Really? It was her idea? Why then, it must be good!*

Which is to say, if you found this book at the bottom of a remainder bin for $1.99, don't blame me. It's Peggy's fault.

Having secured a high-powered Canadian book contract, I immediately called my brother Ian. He's the creator of Toronto's improvised soap opera *Sin City,* and he is just about as close to the compleat Canadian as you can get. This is a guy who wears plaid flannel shirts because he honestly thinks they're fashionable. I called him up and said, "Ian, it's me!" And he said, "Who?" And I said, "Will," and he said, "Will *who?*" and I said, "Will, your brother," and he said, "I have a brother?" and I said, "Is this about the towels I stole from you last time I was out?" and he said, "Oh yeah, I remember you. What do you want?" and I said, "Listen, I was talking to Margaret Atwood the other day—" and he immediately shouted, "Count me in! Whatever it is, count me in!" "Have you actually read Margaret Atwood?" I asked. "It doesn't matter," he said. "It's Margaret Atwood. Count me in!"

[Enough banter. Get to the point—Ed]

Now, at this juncture you may very well be asking yourself a few questions (beyond "Why did I blow $1.99 on this?"). For example, you might be wondering—aloud, so as to justify the use of quotation marks—"Who are you to write such a book?" Well, Ian and I are both Canadians. And, as noted, we are brothers. We have been Canadians our whole lives and, um, did I mention the part about us being Canadians and all?

Not to oversell it or anything, but *How to Be a Canadian* is the greatest guidebook ever written. It will explain everything you'll ever need to know. It will change your life and improve your posture and cure cancer. Every question you could possibly have is answered within these pages. And it comes with an ironclad guarantee! If you are not 100% completely satisfied with this product, our publisher, Scott McIntyre, will personally come to your house and wax your car for you, free of charge, for life! That's how confident we are!

And finally: Ms. Atwood, if you're reading this, I would like say, heart to heart, from one hoser to another, "Thanks, eh?"

WILL FERGUSON

SOME IDEAS ABOUT MARGARET ATWOOD

(In which Ian shamefully confesses his relationship—or lack thereof—with one of Canada's most respected authors)

So I'm sitting at home and the phone rings. Some guy claiming to be my brother is on the line. I'm guessing he wants to borrow money. Again. Or maybe steal some more towels. But no, it turns out that Margaret Atwood (a personal friend of his, it seems) has been "pestering" him with an idea for his next book. And, possibly because he's still feeling bad about the Towel Incident, he's asking me to write it with him. How could I say no?

I quickly cleared my calendar of upcoming meetings and sat down to work. Then, just as I was about to launch into action, a horrible thought occurred to me. Margaret Atwood. Which of her books had I read? Had I read any of her books? I searched my memory, my bookshelves and my permanent record at the Toronto Public Library.

My bookshelves weren't much help, being full mainly of back issues of the *Muskoka Weekly News* and, like, metaphysics and stuff.

My permanent record at the library wasn't any better, though I did discover that they consider me a "difficult" customer, due to the extended period of time I sometimes keep my, well, okay, *their* books out. Who would have guessed how quickly library fines add up? I'd have to donate a kidney to pay for them. Which I won't, having already promised one to Will.

But I did finally recall reading *something* by Atwood. I think it was the one about the dyspeptic future where men had cruelly taken over all aspects of women's lives, forcing them to give birth to children they didn't want and controlling their every action. (I know you're probably expecting a joke about the Alliance Party and Stockwell Day right here, but forget it. That sort of topical, shelf-life humour would never have made it past our sharp-eyed editor.)

So I *had* read an Atwood book: *The Handmaid's Tale*. But. Here's the thing. The only reason I read it was because I had once been forced to sit through a really bad American movie adaptation. It was so bad I attempted to walk out halfway. However, since it was being presented as our Air Canada in-flight movie... I ended up being accused of air rage instead, and I am now banned from Canada's only full-service, full-schedule airline. Since I can't afford

their full-fare prices, it's not that big a loss. It did, however, inspire me to read the book upon which the movie
was based.

I was now ready for my first meeting with Will's publisher, the affable and gnomelike Scott McIntyre. I had
assumed that Mr. McIntyre would want to discuss the
state of Canadian culture and literature, and I was sure
Margaret Atwood's name would come up in conversation.
In preparation, I had even rented the very fine Canadian
movie *Margaret's Museum,* in the mistaken belief that
it was a documentary about her life. It didn't seem to be.
Mind you, I watched it on fast-forward with the sound
muted, so maybe I missed her cameo. (*Note:* Even on fast-
forward with the sound muted, *Margaret's Museum* is inter-
minably long and depressingly morbid.)

As it turned out, Scott didn't want to discuss the Can-
Lit pantheon. He was more concerned with publisher-type
things. "You won't miss your deadline, right?" he said, eyes
wild, voice frantic. "Because the deadline is next week,
and we still haven't seen anything. All we've got is an anecdote from your brother about hobnobbing with Margaret
Atwood. God, I need a drink."

So I squared my shoulders, I looked him dead in the eye,
and I did what writers have been doing to publishers since
Johannes Gutenberg first invented type. I lied through
my teeth. "Scott," I said, "I have been a professional playwright for over ten years. I have never missed a deadline.
Ever. And I don't intend to miss this one." Somewhere, off
in the distance, you could hear the bitter laughter of doz-
ens of stage directors, designers and actors, some of whom
are still waiting for promised revisions to plays now being
studied in theatre history classes.

And what is my point? Do I even have a point? Well, yes. In a country as diverse as this one, a book like ours provides a vital service.

Is it unreasonable to suggest that a book like *How to Be a Canadian* should be required reading for every Canadian, every newcomer, every landed immigrant? And let's not forget refugee claimants, real or imagined. How better to increase our knowledge of ourselves and this great land than by buying just such a book? Actually, I don't want you to buy *such* a book, I want you to buy this one. (Don't cheat by borrowing it from the library; the fines'll kill you.)

IAN FERGUSON

HOW THIS BOOK IS ORGANIZED

This guidebook provides advice on every aspect of Canadian culture, including diet, dating rituals, politics, fashion, etiquette, complex social structures and beer. As such, it contains a wealth of information gathered from fact-filled articles that the authors of this book sort of remember reading somewhere, in a newspaper or something.

Over the last twenty-four months, Will and Ian have crisscrossed the country and interviewed hundreds of Canadians, young and old, coast to coast, in every walk of life—but to be honest, none of those people were much help, so we haven't bothered including anything they said. The single exception is the material about Quebec's dietary habits and driving patterns. Our informant in Quebec is another one of our brothers.* The brother in question is a

---

* There are four Ferguson brothers in total. We're just like the Baldwins. Except that we aren't rich. Or famous. Or constantly being pursued by love-struck, hysterical fans. But other than that, we're just like the Baldwins.

prize-winning composer of classical music who has been living in Montreal for more than a decade, and because of his highly sensitive position within the Montreal arts community, he has asked us not to name him. That would be Sean Ferguson of 2201B Devoir Drive.

You will notice that this guidebook, as well as being crammed full of useful tidbits, also contains many helpful lists. This is because:

A. they are easy to write
B. they give the impression of scientific rigour where none exists
C. you can create humour simply by repeating an item on the list, and
D. they are easy to write

At the end of each chapter we have provided a pithy summary of everything you need to know about the preceding pages. These chapter wrap-ups are meant to help you in much the same manner that students across Canada have been aided and abetted by *Coles Notes*—which, you will recall, routinely reduce any work of literature to the most basic of plot summaries. (*Hamlet?* Guy comes home from college, finds out his father is dead and his mother is married to his uncle. Lots of swordfights. The end.)

When you're reading these brief summary sections, remember that they can also be used to help you with your attempts at assimilation. So you can skip most of the material in *How to Be a Canadian* but still be prepared to contribute to sophisticated cocktail party chatter when the subject of this book comes up (as we know it will). No one will be the wiser. So don't let a lack of time or initiative prevent you from purchasing and enjoying this fine work of insightful Canadiana.

We also wanted to include lots of cool pie charts and maps and diagrams, but then we noticed the clause in our contract that states the cost of any illustrations will be "covered by the authors." So we decided to go with a stark, understated approach instead, without a bunch of distracting graphics. I mean, do you really *need* a map of Canada in a book about Canada? Well, yes, actually. But try telling that to our cheapskate publisher. Gnomelike, our ass.

1

INTRODUCTION

How to Find Canada on a Map*

. . . .

*(map not included)

*C*ANADA IS a very large nation, most of which is above water. A "continental cornice stone" located between Greenland and Irkutsk, Canada is where the bombs will land when the U.S. Strategic Defence Initiative takes effect.

GOVERNMENT

The capital of Canada is Bay Street. The government, however, is located in Ottawa, a sunny, semi-tropical city on the banks of the St. Lawrence River. We think. Much beloved by poets and painters, Ottawa is a city of canals. It is often compared to Venice. In fact, among certain jet-setting circles, Venice is now known as "the Ottawa of Europe."

ECONOMY

The main product manufactured in Canada is snow. Canada also exports sulphate, bauxite, nitrate, alunite and cellulite (winter only: *see* "Florida"). Canada has many other vibrant industries as well, which you are more than welcome to look up. In an encyclopedia. Or maybe an almanac.

CURRENCY

The unit of currency in Canada is the Canadian dollar, also known as El Peso del Norte. Canadians affectionately refer to their dollar as "the loonie," because there is a picture of a large crazed woman on it.

Two loonies = one toonie
Two toonies = about 50¢ U.S.

POPULATION

There are 30,000,000 people in Canada—all of whom have, at some point, frozen their tongues to the side of a chainlink fence or flagpole. Even though their mothers told them not to. Indeed, at any given time of the year, it is winter somewhere in Canada and someone, somewhere, is stuck to a flagpole. "Hap me, hap me. Tumbuddy, pwease hap me."

AVERAGE I.Q.

See above.

LANGUAGE(S)

Canadians speak French and English, often at the same time. *Trayz sophisticated, n'est pah?* Known far and wide as master linguists, Canadians excel in particular at translating cereal boxes. Often, when the U.N. needs a cereal box translated, they call in the Canadians, who parachute out of stealth bombers clutching boxes of Capitaine Crounche and K de Special. In a situation unique among the world's nations, English Canadians know what the French is for "riboflavin," "niacin" and "part of a complete breakfast." And vice versa. English Canadians don't know what riboflavin *is* (no one does), but they do sort of know what it looks like in French. And vice versa.

SIZE

In Canada, *size matters.* Everything is very big in Canada, from the size of the deficit to the girth of Canadian buttocks—as can be observed while standing in line at any I.G.A. or Safeway checkout counter. (Scientists have cited the generous backside of the Canadian consumer as proof positive that the universe is expanding—and at an exponential rate.) Big mountains, big skies, big helpings and massive coronaries: in Canada, every day is a Supersized™ day!

Canada is the Big Gulp of nations. It's enormous: larger than Donovan Bailey's ego (remember him?), larger than a Shawinigan bank loan, larger than an MP's pension fund.

Note: It is considered bad manners to point out to Canadians that, although their country is indeed very large, more than 50% of it is permanently frozen. This is the "We burned your fries so we gave you extra" school of customer satisfaction. As in: "Sure, most of your land is an uninhabited frozen wasteland—but you've got lots of it!" Memo from God: *I froze half your country, so I gave you extra.*

POPULATION DENSITY

Although large, Canada is sparsely populated. Very sparsely. With so much land and so few people, the ratio is, oh, we don't know, something like one person for every 100 square miles or something. Someone should look that up.

The point is this: In Canada you are entitled to your 100 square miles of land per person, so don't be shy! Stride out into a farmer's field or a stretch of forest and stake your claim. "This spot and the 100 miles that surround it belong to me!"

Rest assured, this is perfectly legal. In fact, it was by just such a process that Canada itself was first taken. A Frenchman named Jacques Cartier showed up and stuck a cross in the ground and claimed all of Canada for France. In Newfoundland, Humphrey Gilbert simply read a proclamation and, zim-zam, the whole shebang belonged to England. In the Arctic, Joseph-Elzéar Bernier fired his gun nineteen times in the air and claimed the world's largest archipelago for Canada. See how easy it is?

So go ahead and plant a cross or fire a gun or read a proclamation, and those 100 square miles are all yours.

COAT OF ARMS

From the official description of the Royal Pooh-bah Colonial Mind-Set Heraldry Association:

> Canada's armorial arms consists of a beaver resplendent beneath a thistle apparent, adjoined by a lion rampant, a muskrat lethargic and maples redundant, bordered with guile supercilious and garlands uncertain... *unless* it is on display in a Governor General's procession in a month beginning on a Tuesday, *if* the procession is preceded by a duke or nobleman of lesser bloodline, but *not* by a standard-bearer of a third-order gene recessive, in which case the pattern is reversed and all bets are off.

Ah yes, our great British heritage.

NATIONAL EMBLEM

Canada's national emblem is a fallen leaf (*see also* Toronto). And no, the Canadian flag does not look like a giant nose-bleed, so put that thought out of your mind right now.

OFFICIAL ROLE MODEL

The Russians have a bear, the Brits a lion and the Americans a mighty eagle. In Canada, the national animal is a beaver. Renowned for its hard work, even temper, industrious nature and—oh, who are we kidding. The beaver is a forty-pound water rat whose most heroic trait is that he thinks to slap his tail and warn his buddies before he runs away. And cripes, it's not like Canadians were short on choices. The country is filled with nobler, more awe-inspiring animals. The timber wolf. The grizzly bear. The mountain lion. The woodland bison. Hell, even a caribou or a muskox would have been better than a buck-toothed, webbed-toed, waddle-happy rodent. But *noooo,* when Canada's national animal was finally made official in 1975, it was the beaver that was chosen.

> *Question:* If a lion, an eagle and a beaver were pitted against one another, wouldn't that be cool?

Canadians love their furry mascot. Love him to pieces. Literally. Provinces like Manitoba spend hundreds of thousands of dollars every year blowing up dams, dynamiting beavers and sending in bulldozers in a desperate attempt to stop the soggy little pest (or, rather, "proud national symbol"). In fact, Manitoba recently upped its bounty on beavers, with some communities offering another $20 a head on top of the current $15. (Idea for a fast-paced CBC action show: *The Bounty Hunter, Manitoba-style.* "He always gets his *Castor canadensis!*")

A true story from our bulging files on beaver crimes: In 1992, a beaver dam flooded train tracks northeast of Thunder Bay, derailing a train and killing two crew members. (Idea for a fast-paced CBC docudrama: *Killer Water Rats: Evil or Just Plain Bad?*)

NATIONAL ANTHEM

The national anthem of Canada goes like this:

> Da da da da DA DAAA
> Da da da da DA
> Da da da DA da da da
> Da da da da DAAA . . .
> Da da

It's true. The theme song from *Hockey Night in Canada* has more resonance among Canadians than any other piece of music. Even better, it's easy to remember, consisting as it does of a single word.*

It is also a vast improvement on Canada's official or "real" national anthem, "O Canada," which has been revised, rewritten and recast repeatedly by Parliament. This is the anthem you will hear being mumbled proudly at public venues across our great land. First lesson as a newcomer to Canada: Whatever you do, *do not learn the words*

---

* "Da."

to "O Canada"! Nothing will mark you as an outsider more quickly. Canadians don't know the words to their national anthem, and neither should you.

Mind you, it's no wonder Canadians get tripped up, when you consider how often the lyrics have been tinkered with to make them "politically correct" and "socially acceptable." For example, the original lyrics went:

> O Canada! Our home and <u>native</u> land!
> Something something something
> In all thy <u>sons</u> command

The revised version:

> Louie, Louie
> Whoa oh-oh, we gotta go, yeah yeah
>   yeah yeah yeah yeah
> Louie, Louie

"OFFICIAL" NATIONAL ANTHEM

In keeping with the dualistic nature of Canadian society, there are not one but *two* official versions of "O Canada." No, not English and French, but rather Protestant and Catholic.

Here are actual quotes taken from Canada's national anthem: first the Protestant version, and then the Catholic version. (Technically, only the first verse in either is official, but the lines below are real nonetheless.)

The Protestant version describes Canada as "a land of hope for those who toil," emphasizes duty ("we stand on guard!"), and includes the lines:

> Help us to find, O God, in Thee,
> A lasting, rich reward,
> As waiting for the Better Day

The Catholic version is, as might be expected, more fun than the Protestant version. It emphasizes glory and history, with the opening lines *"O Canada, terre de nos aïeux/ Ton front est ceint de fleurons glorieux"* ("O Canada! Land of our ancestors/Your brow is wreathed with glorious garlands"). It ends with the cry *"Pour le Christ et le Roi!"* ("For Christ and King!") and includes the lines:

> *Car ton bras sait porter l'épée,*
> *Il sait porter la croix!*
> *Ton histoire est une épopée*
> *Des plus brillants exploits.*

Which translates directly as:

> Your arm knows how to carry the sword,
> It knows how to carry the cross.
> Your history is an epic
> Of the most brilliant exploits

Is it any wonder Canadians are confused? All together now! *Louie, Louie* . . .

HISTORY

Canadian history is incredibly boring. For example: In the 1600s the French settlers waged a frontier guerilla war against the Iroquois Confederacy, and later, when the

English moved in, a vast imperial conflict ranged from Newfoundland to the frozen shores of Hudson Bay. Swashbuckling French privateers battled it out with British redcoats, the Acadians were sent into exile, and, in 1759, the two European powers clashed headlong on the Plains of Abraham. No sooner had New France been conquered than the frontier boiled over and the Americans invaded Canada. They were fought back only to regroup and re-attack in 1812. Inland, the adventure continued, as explorers followed treacherous whitewater rivers through the mountains and all the way to the Pacific. A dangerous standoff was ignited on the Pacific Coast when Spain, Britain and the United States jostled for position and control. At one point, it came to the brink of war over a single, marauding pig. In 1837, armed rebellions were launched in Upper and Lower Canada, only to be crushed by the British government. In 1867, the northern British colonies were cobbled together to form a new dominion, largely as a defensive move to counter the U.S. Civil War, which threatened to spill over the border at any moment. A vast transcontinental railway was built from sea to sea, and an armed Metis rebellion raged in the Northwest. Gold was discovered in the Yukon, one of the most remote and inhospitable regions on earth, and thousands made the trek north in search of wealth and glory. The West was won, the Arctic islands were taken, and in the skies of Europe above the trenches of World War I, Canada provided more and better fighter pilots than any other nation. The Great Depression wreaked havoc, the prairies turned into a dustbowl, the world was plunged headlong into war again, and Canadians came under heavy fire in Hong Kong, Dieppe and Italy and on the beaches of Normandy. In 1945, the Cold War began when a Soviet agent defected in Ottawa, bringing with him evidence of Communist penetration deep within—ah, but why go on? Like we said, the history of Canada is so dull. It's all just murder, mayhem and massacres.

Fortunately, Canada's academic historians and well-intentioned educators have picked up the ball. Who needs heroes and exiles and great campaigns for justice? *Boooorring!* Why should Canadians know who their leaders were? Why should they be familiar with the key battles and major turning points? That's so outdated.

Instead, we now have "social history." Which of course isn't really history at all. Regular history is about cause and effect. Social history is about endless details and accumulated minutiae. It isn't so much history as it is "historical sociology." Hint: If you see the words "working-class conditions" or "an examination of gender roles," you are reading social history (i.e., sociology). And boy oh boy, kids today can't get enough of it! "Forget John A. Macdonald and the conquest of a continent," they cry. "We want to know more about the social conditions of eighteenth-century textile workers!"

Canadian history is no longer about "people" (as in, individuals). It is about "peoples." Note the telltale use of the plural. Whenever you see the word "peoples" in a title, you know you are in for some excellent, rip-roaring, social-demographic, ethnically sensitive, gender-correct sociological studies! So, get yourself a blanket and a big ol' pillow and settle yourself down for a nice long snooze.

CLIMATE

Canada has two anthems, two languages and two versions of its history. There is the assumption that Canada has only two seasons as well: Winter and Not Winter. But this isn't true.

In fact, Canada has no fewer than *six* distinct seasons: Tax; Hockey; More Hockey; Still More Hockey; Summer (also known as the July Long Weekend, also known as "Was that it?"); and finally Good God, Isn't the Hockey Season Over by Now?!

In defiance of both Einstein and the space-time continuum, hockey in Canada now lasts sixteen months a year. Both the tax season and summer have been swamped by hockey—and that's just regular hockey. The playoffs stretch things out even further. Glaciers move faster than the standard NHL season. There are teams with sideburns and disco hairdos still circling the ice trying to finish off the 1974 season. So if you are going to be a Canadian, you will have to get used to this. Hockey is the Muzak of Canadian society. It's always there, in the background, like radiation or white noise. "Da da da da DA DAA . . ."

CHAPTER I SUMMARY: WHAT YOU'VE LEARNED SO FAR

Canada is a big, cold country. Most of the people in Canada live as close as they can to the U.S. border, where they huddle together for warmth. It you want to appear Canadian, all you have to do is tuck a beaver under your arm and stroll along humming the *Hockey Night in Canada* theme song.

But if you truly want to know what being a Canadian is all about, wait until the next really, really, *really* cold day and then go outside and lick the nearest flagpole or bicycle rack. No, don't worry. It'll be fun. Come on. We've all done it. Sure, it's going to hurt, but it will also give you an important insight into a shared Canadian cultural experience. Think of it as an initiation. Your mouth will eventually stop bleeding, but the memory will last a lifetime.

CANADA:
A RICH TAPESTRY

(who to hate and why)

. . . .

How to
Mingle with Canadians

HOW TO MEET CANADIANS

*T*HE NATURAL habitat of Canadians is the shopping mall. Canadians are timid, but they will respond if approached. The best way, we find, is to offer them a handful of seeds whilst speaking softly in a calm but firm voice.

As noted, Canada has a very low population-to-area ratio. So low, in fact, that you may be wondering how you will ever meet any actual Canadians. This is an understandable concern. If, as the demographics suggest, Canadians were scattered out one per every 100 miles (or, more accurately, every 86.4 hectares per litre), it would be very difficult to make contact with them. But fortunately, Canadians tend to clump themselves together in places known, for lack of a better word, as "cities." (These cities are spaced out every 100 miles or so, natch.) In the province of Manitoba alone, for example, more than half the population lives in one large mega-city: Winnipeg. And they all hang out at the mall.

Indeed, many of Canada's shopping malls have cities conveniently attached. Mall technology (MT) has reached its highest level in Western Canada (defined as "that part of Canada which is not Toronto and which doesn't speak French or catch fish"). The city of Edmonton, for example, is now working on a retractable roof that will enclose the entire community in a single climate-controlled environment. If you have been to Edmonton, you will know why.

The city of Calgary, meanwhile, has a series of hamster tubes connecting the buildings in its downtown core, allowing its citizens to scurry from shop to shop without ever having to face the elements or breathe non-filtered air. Many office blocks in Calgary have added large rotating wheels for office workers to run inside of, providing hours of entertainment—and exercise! In Calgary, this is known as Plus 15. In Winnipeg, it's called the Skywalk. In Halifax, the Pedway.

Montreal, for its part, has an entire rabbit warren of subterranean tunnels. Also known as "cashacombs," these underground shopping plazas have names like Place du Canada, Place du Québec, Place du Québec avec Canada, and Canada à bas! (East Island only).

HOW TO INSULT CANADIANS
(AND OTHER VALUABLE SOCIAL SKILLS)

If you truly wish to mingle with Canadians, you will need to go out into your community and make contact with your neighbours in order to insult them. After all, feeling offended is a popular Canadian pastime. (Sample sentence: "As a _____, I find that offensive.")

We'll start with the basics: regional identity. Every region in Canada hates/resents/looks down upon every other region—often at the same time. So, it is very important that you know the local "lingo." You can't go around calling Albertans "herring chokers" or Maritimers "rig pigs." It just won't do.

Below is a list of regional insults and epithets. These are the VERY WORST THINGS you can possibly call someone. Simply employ these japes and watch the fun begin!

On the West Coast: "tree-hugging"; "granola munching"; "Commie"
In Western Canada: "red-neck"; "fundamentalist"; "Nazi"
In Toronto: "*not* from a world-class city"
Anywhere else in Canada: "Torontonian"
In Quebec (when addressing English speakers): "*tête carrée*"; "*maudits Anglais*"
In Quebec (when addressing French speakers): "Canadian"
In the Maritimes: "Newfie"
In Newfoundland: "Maritimer"

Note: Newfoundlanders hate to be referred to as "Maritimers." As any Newfoundlander will tell you—again and again if you let them—they are most definitely *not* Maritimers. They are from the "Atlantic provinces." And where are the Atlantic provinces located? In the Maritimes.

You will soon realize how useful these terms can be in increasing both the range of your descriptions and the depth of your discussions. For example, say you are discussing a film with someone from Vancouver:

Vancouver-type person: "I thought that movie was pretty good."
Your original reply: "I disagree."

Now, here is the revised and improved version:

Vancouver-type person: "I thought that movie was pretty good."
Revised statement: "I disagree, you granola-munching, tree-hugging Commie."

Or perhaps somebody makes the following statement: "The current alienation of Western Canada is the result of long-term under-representation due to this country's first-past-the-gate electoral system of government. To correct this imbalance, greater regional representation is needed."

The proper response to such a statement is: "You redneck fundamentalist Nazi."

You can see how much this sort of thing contributes to Canada's national dialogue.

CANADA'S OFFICIAL DRESS CODE

Insults, like tears, are not enough. To fully blend in with the local inhabitants, you will need to dress like a Canadian. Some suggestions include saris, kimonos, Jamaican tie-dyes, Peruvian ponchos, Indonesian sandals, Albanian sweaters and brightly coloured fez caps. Anything goes, and the more self-contradictory, the better.

Multicultural chaos is the single most exhilarating aspect of being Canadian. You know how "fusion cuisine" takes perfectly good food from different cultures (say, Italian ice cream and Guatemalan chilies) and then mashes it together to create a new cuisine that is, in direct contradiction of Gestalt theory, decidedly *less* than the sum of its parts? Well, the Canadian notion of postmodern identity is pure fusion. So mix and match as much as you like. The less consistent, the better. Wear your sombrero as a yarmulka. Wear combat boots and fatigues to demonstrate your militantly held pacifist beliefs. Join an anarchist club! (As long as you conform to the established anarchist dress code.) Don your Doc Martens while attending an elegant cocktail soiree to raise money for the homeless: "Doc Martinis for everyone!" Welcome to the brave new postmodern world.

And no, it isn't silly. It's Canadian.

Of course, you may decide to poo-poo the entire po-mo mu-mu. Postmodern eclecticism in Canada is, after all, much like UFOs or worthwhile federal initiatives. You hear a lot about them, but you never actually see one firsthand. Real Canadians dress like, well, like Canadians.

Despite a handful of famous Canadian clothing designers (and, really, the only one we can think of off the top of our heads is Alfred Sung), the reality is that Canadians don't pay much attention to fashion. For years, the national uniform was fairly straightforward: a pair of jeans, a plaid shirt and woollen socks. Sure, some of us had to occasionally put on a necktie or pantyhose, but that was only temporary, work-related camouflage. When we went out on the town, we switched back into our *real* clothes.

Like the Mao jacket in Communist China, the Canadian plaid shirt provided the proletariat with a strong sense of collective identity. It was comforting. You didn't have to make any decisions, and other than a brief experiment with flared jeans in the mid-1970s, the outfit remained exactly the same for decades—until Neil Young came along. Neil's international success caused our national uniform to be adopted by everybody from grunge rockers in Seattle to lesbian social workers in Glasgow.

Now that the typical Canadian uniform is worn world-wide, it is no longer the instant identifier it used to be. What, then, are we to do? Our suggestion is for Canadians to dress the way they did when they were kids, back when their mothers were dressing them. Start off with a layer of long johns (make sure they're made out of that golfball dimple fabric that leaves your thighs looking like Belgian waffles), add a pair of hand-me-down GWGs that are thirty sizes too big ("You'll grow into them, dear, we'll just hitch them up a bit, say nipple level . . . Oh, that looks smart! And now you have a breast pocket and a hip pocket all in one"), put on a pair of nylon ski pants (the kind that produce a loud scratching noise whenever you walk), then throw on a pair of mittens and a parka. And don't forget your boots!*

Finally, top your outfit off with a toque. The standard Canadian toque is designed to keep your head warm, but nobody has ever figured out what the pompom on top is for. It doesn't add to your warmth, and, when you pull up the hood of your parka, the pompom throws your entire centre of gravity off, causing you to lean forward so far that you're looking directly at the fake buckles on your skidoo boots. (And what was the deal with those fake buckles anyway?

---

* Remember to pick skidoo boots with fake buckles on the front, the kind with the outer nylon shell and the inner felt-liner sock. This will get your morning off to an exciting start as you attempt to put on each boot in one movement. It can't be done. You will have to sit down, pull off the nylon outer layer, put on the liner, and then slide the outer portion over it. And then you'll have to repeat the entire procedure for the other foot. Every kid in Canada has done this. Several times.

Was *anyone* ever fooled by them?) A word of warning regarding toques and the maintenance of: You can't cut the pompom off. It's like a support beam for the toque. Cut it off and the whole thing disintegrates. Weird, eh?

So. There you go: a uniform that practically shouts "I'm a Canadian." And the best part about it is, nobody else in the entire world will want to copy our style this time. Unless Neil decides to change his image . . .

CANADA'S OFFICIAL HAIRCUT

When singer Billy Ray Cyrus moved to Canada,* some people wondered what the attraction had been. The clean air? The mountains majestic? The many an achy-breaky heart? No. The answer was simple. He came because of the hair.

In northern U.S. states such as Michigan and Minnesota, it is known simply as "the Canadian." In Canada it is called the "mullet" or, more commonly, "the hockey haircut." It is the National Hairdo of Canada, a blend of long and short, conservative and rebel, silly and stupid, Ray and Cyrus.

How does one concoct a "hockey haircut"? It isn't easy. Like Canada itself, the hairstyle is a blend of competing urges, embodying both compromise and a profound duality. The hair is cut short over the skull but left long in the back. When done properly, it should look like a cropped porcupine wearing a cape.

Note from Ian: In my never-ending pursuit as an older brother to embarrass my younger siblings, I would like to note

* Which is, of course, one of the signs of the Apocalypse.

that Will is sporting a classic "hockey haircut" in the author photo at the back of his recent book *I Was a Teenage Katima-victim!*

Will replies: *Au contraire.* The book to which you refer—available in all the better bookstores, I might add—does not in fact contain a photo of a "hockey haircut." It is, rather, a wry postmodern Gen-X commentary on cultural identity and the tyranny of style.

Ian: Or lack thereof.

Will: *Mom!* Ian's picking on me!

Ian: Neener, neener! You got a haircut! You got a hockey haircut!

Will: Shut up! Mom, make him stop!

Mom (from the top of the stairs): Do I have to come down there and knock your heads together?

Will: [sullen silence]

Ian (whispering): Neener, neener.

CHAPTER 2 SUMMARY: WHAT YOU'VE LEARNED SO FAR

To blend in amongst Canadians, you first must A. locate them, B. dress like them, and C. learn to insult them in a casual, carefree manner. Fortunately, all three objectives are fairly easy. Especially the last one.

Canadians are very easy to insult. Case in point: Ian was once on an elevator in downtown Toronto, and the only other occupant was a dear old lady who kept asking him if he knew her grandson (who, as it turned out, lived in Vancouver). The elevator doors were about to close when a smartly dressed young woman came running up. The elderly lady immediately stopped the doors with her cane and called out, "Come on in, sweetie." The younger woman got on and glared at the older woman. "I think that was very rude," she said. True story. Ian was agog. What could this well-tailored, ill-mannered woman possibly have to be insulted about? He waited until the grandma, obviously flustered, got off on her floor, and then asked the wounded party what had set her off. Well, it turns out that although her family has been in Canada since Christ went down with the *Titanic,* her last name was Svenson or something. She was of Swedish extraction, you see, and she thought the old woman was making a racial slur. "Sweetie/Swedie." Get it? And no, we aren't kidding.

So, hell, Ian did the only thing he could do. Which was to tell this woman to take her Ikea-buying, herring-eating, Abba-playing, sauna-sweating, meatball-making ass back to wherever it was she came from. Which, as it turned out, was Mississauga. Those damn Swedes. We let them in, give them jobs, and the next thing you know they're taking over. This used to be a great country until those damned "Swedies" moved in.

3

A CROSS-CANADA TOUR

. . . .

How to Get Lost

*C*ANADA: WHERE mighty rivers flow and majestic wheat fields blow (in the "Flanders Fields" sense only*). A land of stunning scenery and awe-inspiring natural beauty.

The best way to see this scenery is from the window of an airplane at 30,000 feet while slightly sloshed on high-altitude alcohol. As a fledgling Canadian, you may, however, be stricken with "road fever," symptoms of which include the overwhelming urge to lock yourself in a car for weeks on end, hunched over a steering wheel and enjoying a splendid view of asphalt and the back-end mudflaps of Winnebagos—a vista even more enchanting than that of an airplane wing!

THE RULES OF THE ROAD: HOW TO DRIVE LIKE A CANADIAN

If you plan on crossing this great land of ours by car, you will first need to become familiar with some of the quaint

---

* You see, there was this whole controversy when they wanted to quote from "In Flanders Fields" on Canadian money, over whether they should change "blow" to "grow," but then—oh, never mind.

driving customs you may encounter along the way. Many of these customs, if done properly, will kill you.

Obtaining a driver's licence in Canada is apparently quite easy, because you will see behind the wheel everyone from kindergarten students out on day passes to cigar-smoking chimpanzees zipping along at twice the speed limit, veering back and forth across lanes as they unfold accordion road maps or argue with their spouse or fiddle compulsively with radio knobs and—OH MY GOD! THEY'RE COMING RIGHT AT US!

So go to it! Save up those candy wrappers, send in those coupons, and you too can have your very own authentic Canadian Driver's Licence—as long as you agree to respect the following rules of the road. (Offer void in Quebec.)

The Maritime Headlight-Flick

This custom is so incredible it has been profiled on *Unexplained Mysteries* and *Believe It or Not!* Unlike in virtually every other region of Canada, in the Maritimes merging lanes is not a battle to the death. No one is ever in a hurry here, and this shows up in the neighbourly way people drive. Fire trucks answering a four-alarm blaze will smile and wave you in ahead of them. (Compare that to Calgary, where the city's competitive and notoriously impatient drivers will routinely try to pass each other in the A&W drive-thru lane. There is more testosterone among drivers in Calgary, male and female alike, than in any other city. *Official motto of Calgary drivers:* "C'mon, c'mon, c'mon. Go go go go GO!")

While living in New Brunswick, Will was confounded by the way drivers would flick their headlights at him when he was waiting to turn left across their lane. It took him forever to realize that this light flick meant, "You go on ahead. I'll wait until you have completed your turn before I continue through the intersection, even though I do technically have the right of way. But who's keeping track, eh? After you, I insist."

Is that bizarre or what? It goes against every theory of social evolution ever put forward and is (further) proof that Maritimers are alien pod people in human disguise. Courtesy? *On the road??* It's not natural.

The Montreal Manoeuvre

Remember *Cannonball Run?* That was nothing. Come to Montreal if you want to see a real Death Race 2000. Montreal drivers are famous in the same way that Japanese war pilots were famous: there is something disturbing and yet—somehow—oddly compelling about unbridled suicidal impulses.

Back in the eighties, when Will was living in St. Canut, north of the city, Montreal pedestrians were still a bit wary; they would wait at a corner until a good-sized crowd had formed before forcing their way across the street. It was a "gang jaywalk," and it gave pedestrians a certain *esprit de corps,* the kind of "us against them" attitude that has kept Montreal going all these years.

Will's brother Sean, however, assures him that this behaviour has changed. "Nobody waits for a crowd to form any more, and nobody waits for a light to change. In fact, they don't even wait for a break in the traffic."

Today, the quintessential Montreal manouevre is to walk *really* slowly across Ste. Catharine—against the light—and when an approaching car honks, to slow your pace down EVEN MORE in order to give the driver the evil eye. Then, as the car passes, you bend down low, so the driver can see you in the rear-view mirror, and you give them the finger along with a *mangez de la merde* look.

"You have to see it to appreciate it," says Sean admiringly. "It's very fluid. A kind of street-theatre ballet."

The Toronto Toreador

It is something that has baffled scientists to no end. English Canadians, deferential to the point of neurosis and apologetic to the point of self-caricature, are suddenly transformed into wolverine wannabes—not the comic-book character, but *actual* wolverines—the moment they strap themselves into a car. Nowhere is this truer than in Toronto.

The day will come when every Torontonian will be equipped with their own personal motorcade of siren-shrieking police escorts, thus allowing every single person to run every single red light. Which is more or less what happens now.

In Toronto, traffic lights are interpreted in the following manner:

Green: "Don't stop!"
Yellow: "Faster! Faster!"
Red: "Screw 'em, they deserved to die."

There is something about the sight of a yellow traffic light that enrages Torontonians. It's provocative, a kind of amber-coloured bullfighter's cape. A yellow light in Toronto is considered an affront. "Here I am, going Somewhere Important, and this light—this mere traffic light—is telling me I must pause. Puh-leeze."

When faced with the sheer effrontery of a yellow signal, the correct response in Toronto is *never* to slow down, even if you are two blocks away. No, the correct response is to grip the wheel and plunge both feet onto the gas pedal with as much force as possible, accelerating wildly. If your timing is accurate and your aim is true, you should be able to fly through the intersection at 100 miles an hour *at the exact moment the light turns red*. Physicists using sophisticated radium crystal clocks have been unable to replicate this feat. It's a matter of skill and pride on the part of Toronto drivers, and further evidence of their world-class status. After all, they run red lights in L.A. too, right?

The Winnipeg Wetsuit

Winnipeg was under water the last time we went through, so we're afraid we don't have any tips on driving there, except to recommend an amphibious vehicle of some sort. *Note:* It is considered bad manners to say, "You call this a flood? Hell, I was in Saguenay back in '96 and the buildings were being swept away. Now *that* was a flood!"

The Vancouver Slalom

There are no roads in British Columbia. There are only corners joined together. And nowhere is this truer than in Vancouver. In this city, pedestrians, even those within clearly marked crosswalks—*especially* those within clearly marked crosswalks—are viewed not as nuisances to be avoided but as obstacles to be overcome. Rising to the challenge, Vancouver drivers will attempt to weave through these pedestrians without knocking any over—

and, here's the fun part, *without ever applying the brakes.*
Swoosh, swoosh: downtown slalom. Pedestrians, in turn,
try to keep things interesting by crisscrossing the streets at
random, like neutrons in a particle accelerator. They cross
the street like this because, being from Vancouver, they
naturally have a sense of entitlement. Either that or they're
stoned.

CHOOSING YOUR CHARIOT

It is important to select a vehicle suited to the type of environment where you will do most of your driving. If you live
in the city and plan to do your driving in an urban environment, for example, you will need to get a rugged Sports
Utility Vehicle (suv). These are the hardy outdoor vehicles
that can often be seen in television commercials climbing
up mountainsides or riding logs down whitewater rapids.
Sometimes they are pursued by cougars as well.

In the real world, you won't actually *see* any suvs climbing up the sides of mountains, but you will see them
attempting to parallel park on downtown streets. We say
"attempting to" because in the entire history of the world,
no suv has ever successfully completed a parallel park.
Back and forth, back and forth, lurching in, lurching out: it
can go on for days.

Known as "the mighty T-Rex of the car kingdom" (giant
lumbering body, tiny little brain), the suv is ideal for city
driving and suburban commutes. A business executive trying to back up in an suv is a quintessentially Canadian
sight.

If you live out in the country, on the other hand, you
will need a Big-Assed Luxury Car (BLC) about a mile wide.

Something that really kicks up the gravel. A Lincoln or a Caddy. Something big enough to haul bales in. You know, something suitable for the rural lifestyle.

Okay, you have your vocabulary and you have your vehicle—it's time to hit the road. Here, then, is a province-by-province guide to your adopted homeland. Have fun! Play safe! And don't forget to write.

HITTING THE ROAD

NEWFOUNDLAND: "Land of Sex and Liars"

Location: Somewhere out there in the fog. Damned if we can find it.

Formal Name: "Newfoundland"

Pronounced: "Newfoundland"*

Main Industries: It used to be fish. Now it's, um, well, other stuff. You know.

Cultural History: Yes.

Genuine Affection for Mainlanders: No.

Provincial Motto: "Buddy dere is on'a inside fer sum fine tinkin' wit' a tacker fer d'gulley, eh bys?"

No, no, no. We're just kidding. Newfoundlanders aren't all a bunch of goofy grinning outport fishermen wearing rubber boots and no upper plates. For example, many Newfoundlanders don't have lower plates either. "Buddy dere is askin' for it!"

Newfoundland was first settled by surly Vikings and Irish fishermen. The Vikings had the good sense to leave.

---

* Or, as it is known on the mainland: "NOO-fan-lin," "Nu-FIN-lun," "Newf-and-LIND," and so on.

As England's first overseas colony, Newfoundland is also where the British Empire was born. Conversation comes naturally to Newfoundlanders and, being a people of the sea, their talk often centres around whale oil. As in: "Whale oil beef hooked!"

In every national survey ever taken, Newfoundlanders rank—far and away—as having the most sex of any Canadians. Which is to say, if you telephone Newfoundlanders at random and ask them questions about their sex lives, they will lie to you. "Oh, jeez, sure. Me and the missus go at it every day like a pair of wild raccoons, don't we, hon? How often? Oh, two or three times a day, at least. Usually before breakfast. It's true, it is. I swear on my mother's grave. Thank you. Oh, you're more than welcome. Call again anytime. Tah!" These same surveys indicate that Newfoundlanders are also the *friendliest* people in Canada. Of course they're friendly. They want to have sex with you.

As Canada's easternmost province, Newfoundland is where the sun first rises on Canada. Not that the sun is usually visible. They'll just have to take our word for it. Newfoundland is in its own world and its own time zone. The Trans-Canada Highway both begins and ends at St. John's, after which you have to turn around and come back. The provincial flower eats bugs. Really. The weather is cold and wet (though also, on occasion, wet and cold). The currency is in doubt. The tack is hard. The food is fried. The water is salt. The humour is ubiquitous, and the music is raucous. (Imagine two alleycats locked in a duel to the death, and you have the standard Newfoundland fiddle solo.) Cape Breton is not a part of Newfoundland. But it should be. *Newfoundland: Proudly holding on to Labrador just to annoy Quebec since 1927!*

NOVA SCOTIA: "Land of Dreamers and Doers and Schemers and Schooners—and Let's Not Forget Ashley MacIsaac!"

Buried Treasure: *Yes!!*

Really?: No.

Location: Out east somewhere.

Shape: Sort of sausagelike.

Provincial Motto: "Come for the sunshine, stay for the rain!"

Really? *Rain?*: Yes.

Heavy rain?: Sometimes.

Heavy, wet, cold Atlantic rain with waves as big as the one in that *Perfect Storm* movie what tipped over them fishermen from Gloucester—who, we might add, got their sorry-assed schooner butts kicked by the *Bluenose* way back when?: Yes.

Yellow Nor'westers as a Fashion Statement: Yes.

Rubber Fetish: Possibly.

Welcome to Canada's "Ocean Playground," where the waters are always a balmy 2°. Nova Scotia is part of Canada's "Celtic connection," and as such it is home to the Highland Games, or "Braemar," where Scots Canadians gather every year to honour their great Scottish "heritage" (most of which involves cross-dressing and porridge). They celebrate said heritage by dressing in clashing plaids and throwing heavy objects into the air.

Cape Breton Island (joined to the mainland by a majestic causeway that is every bit as dramatic as PEI's Confederation Bridge) is a rugged and beautiful land completely infested by Rankins. Cape Breton was once thought to be a heartland of ancient Celtic culture where the locals still spoke Gaelic—but it turns out they were just really, really drunk.

The first European settlers in Nova Scotia were French Acadians, but they left or something. The Acadians were followed by British "redcoats," bright scarlet being a particularly clever colour to wear in forest warfare. (Some officers even went one better and began painting large bull's-eyes directly onto the back of their men's uniforms, such was the cunning of the British military leaders.) The Micmac Indians and the British got along famously, often playing practical jokes on one another and staging wacky ambushes (*see* British bounties; Micmac scalps, offers for).

The largest city in the province is Halifax, or, as the Natives called it, *Chebucto* (literally: "Halifax"), and the main export is comedians, most of whom were originally imported from Newfoundland.

When passing through Nova Scotia, don't forget to visit the picturesque village of Lunenburg and make fun of their accent. (The people of Lunenburg speak with a distinctive "lilt," which they greatly enjoy having mimicked by tourists.) Lunenburg was also the home of the famous *Bluenose* schooner, as seen on Canadian coins. What few people realize, however, is that the portrait of the *Bluenose* that appears on the 10-cent piece is a life-size rendering. Understandably, many visitors to Nova Scotia are a bit disappointed when they first see the *Bluenose* tethered in its harbour.

The noses are blue, the lobsters are bisque, and the basements are dank. Nova Scotia was once the haunt of pirates, thieves, scoundrels and rogues. But don't worry. The pirates are gone now.

PRINCE EDWARD ISLAND: "Not Only Small, but Not Very Big Either"

Size: 4′ × 7′

Description: Diminutive.

Location: It was here a moment ago. Check behind the sofa.

Pet Peeve: Getting headlock noogies from the other provinces.

Tired of: Jokes about how small it is.*

Provincial Motto: "Prince Edward Island: Land of the Mighty Potato! And Lots of Other Exciting Stuff!"

Trees on Provincial Flag: Yes.(What many people don't realize is that the provincial flag of PEI is actually a scale-model map of the island itself. Need help getting around? Bring along a provincial flag for directions.)

The Micmac called it *Abegweit* (literally: "Potatoes again?") but to the early settlers it was simply "home." Come to Prince Edward Island and admire its majestic potato fields, stretching into the distance like so many rows of dirt—only better. Everybody loves PEI, especially the Islanders themselves. In the world view of Islanders, there is Prince Edward Island—and then there is everywhere else. Could be Lima, Peru, or Shediac, New Brunswick. Makes no difference. Both are "off island" and "from away." Islanders are wonderfully kind to strangers, but they can't stand their neighbours. (There's not a lot to do in PEI during the winter, so holding grudges became a popular pastime.) Islanders

---

* For example: PEI is so small that when you plug in your electric razor, the streetcars slow down. If they had streetcars. Which they don't. Why? (Brace yourself for a killer punchline.) Because it's so DAMN SMALL, that's why!

are, however, united by one thing: They all hate Anne of Green Gables.

PEI, you see, is an Orwellian police state run by the Canadian version of Big Brother: Li'l Anne. She is all-seeing and all-knowing and all-powerful. Beware her wrath. The Island is home to *Anne, the Never-Ending Musical,* which you are required by law to attend, and many other exciting attractions as well, such as the Anne of Green Gables Souvenir Store, Anne's Lake of Shining Waters, Anne's Babbling Brook, Anne's Polyp-in-a-Mason-Jar Museum, Anne's Den of Iniquity, Anne's Crack House, and so on.

The other famous Islander is Stompin' Tom Connors. He kind of sings and he sort of stomps his foot. In Canada, this makes him a legend. His cowboy boots are displayed on a pedestal outside the Stompin' Tom Museum in Skinners Pond. (And yes, there really is a Stompin' Tom Museum.) There is also a Potato Museum in the town of O'Leary featuring a towering fourteen-foot statue of . . . *Anne.* No. We're only kidding. The statue is actually that of a giant yam, an error that has caused all sorts of outrage in PEI, where the unofficial motto is: "We don't cotton no yam-eaters around here." In PEI, the food is mashed, the soil is red, the oysters are Malpeque, and the winters are long. PEI is eroding even as we speak, so you better get there fast before—oops, too late.

NEW BRUNSWICK: "A Subsidiary of the Irving Corporation"
Main Source of Income: Lottery tickets.
Irving Gas Stations: On every corner.
Tim Hortons Doughnut Shops: On every other corner.
Giant Lobster Statue: Yes.

Roads without Potholes: No.
Comical Use of "Some" to Mean "Very" or "Truly": Yes.
Food That Isn't Deep-fried: No.
Provincial Motto: "New Brunswick! She's some beautiful."

Welcome to the Land of the Loyalists. Heroically defeated in the American Revolution, the Loyalists are—of course—Canadian icons. (In Canada, being defeated is just about the most glorious achievement you can garner.*) And so, having been courageously beaten and valiantly trounced, the noble Loyalists bravely fled and made their way to . . . the Bahamas. Or at least some of them did. The rest came to New Brunswick. (We didn't exactly get the sharpest Loyalists in the lot, if you get our drift.)

In keeping with this proud tradition of heroic failure, New Brunswick later championed the Bricklin sports car. With its gull-winged doors and sleek body, it was the GREATEST CAR EVER PRODUCED. Except for the fact that it was a lemon. And a boondoggle.

There is much to see and do in New Brunswick! The province is home to the mighty tides of Fundy, where, over an exciting action-packed twelve hours of waiting, you can see the water slowly rise as high as—well, we're not sure. We didn't stick around for it. But we're told it is truly magnificent. And mighty.

New Brunswick is also home of the aptly named Tidal Bore ("Look! A ripple. Quick, get the video camera"), as well as Magnetic Hill, where cars roll uphill. Even more impressive is the nearby *Backwards* Magnetic Hill, where

---

* *See* Quebec.

the laws of gravity are reversed again and cars roll . . . *downhill!*

In Hartland, New Brunswick, you will find the world's longest covered bridge. These bridges, known as "kissing bridges," are found throughout the province—although the Hartland Bridge, at 1,282 feet, is more of a "heavy-petting, quick-foreplay, father-waiting-at-the-other-side, shotgun-wedding" sort of bridge.

Oh yes, we found out what happened to the Acadians. Apparently they went on holiday, to Louisiana or someplace, and when they came back the Loyalists had moved in and taken all their land. So the Acadians killed them. Just kidding. The Acadians moved north into upper New Brunswick, where they now make up a third of the population. New Brunswick is, in essence, Canada in miniature.

The Acadians have been able to protect their culture and assert their identity without referendums, kidnappings or assassinations—much to the chagrin of Quebec separatists. The Acadians did, however, give us Roch Voisine, so they are not completely without blame.

The fog is thick, the tides are high, the bridges are covered, and Red Green is considered a role model. New Brunswick is some good.

QUEBEC: "Bah, Wai!"

Distinct Society: Yes

Really?: Maybe. We're not sure.

Come on. Distinct society, yes or no?: That is correct.

Provincial Motto: *Je me souviens* ("I remember"), meaning, "I remember that, in spite of our differences, the spirit of friendship and cooperation between French and English has enabled us to live together in harmony and prosperity." Or something to that effect.

Catholic Churches Every Ten Paces: Yes.

Tabloid Newspapers with Names Like *Police Splatter!* and *Allô Intestines!*: Yes.

Separatists on the Federal Payroll of Radio Canada: Every ten paces, baby.

Wine with Supper: Yes.

Wine with Lunch: Absolutely!

Wine with Breakfast: Why not?

What are they, a bunch of alcoholics?: Yes.

First off, they don't hate *you*. Not personally. The Québécois hate the federal government—and a mythical place called "the Rest of Canada," which is, apparently, some sort of homogeneous, monolithic whole. That's who they hate. So don't worry about—well, okay, *Bernard Landry* hates you, but other than that, you'll be fine. The Québécois are among the friendliest people in Canada outside of Newfoundland. And yes, their motives are probably the same.

In fact, so welcoming and so considerate are the people of Quebec that the government in Paris is seriously considering revoking Quebec's "French" status. "Kaybek? *Pah!* Zay are not rail French! Zay are impostairs!" (That's how they talk in France.)

Don't let the openness of the Québécois fool you, though. The French Canadians were conquered by the British in 1760, and they have been looking for a rematch ever since. Today, the French Fact in Canada is centred mainly—but by no means entirely—within *la belle province* (literally: "the bell province." What this means exactly, no one knows).

Let's face it. The Québécois are the coolest kids in the playground. They sing louder, dance better, kiss deeper and laugh longer than other Canadians. You're going to love Quebec. It has a certain *savoir faire*. A sort of *joie de vivre*. A carefree *je ne sais quoi*. A kind of *de rigueur, par avion, soup du jour* feeling about it. You'll love it. It's so French.

True, you may run into some trouble if you don't speak the language—and the odds are you don't. Want to find out? The standard guidelines, with which you may already be familiar, are as follows:

Someone who speaks three languages is called: "trilingual"
Two languages: "bilingual"
One language: "English Canadian"

But don't fret! Street signs are easy enough to decipher. For example, many of them use the designation *rue,* which means "street." This is easy to remember if you recall that French is a Latin or "Romance" language, and that romance is dead, which is something you "rue" if you are so heartbroken you get hit by a "truck" while crossing the "street."

Other signs can likewise be translated fairly easily. YIELD, for example, means "No surrender! No retreat! To the death!" and ARRÊT, apparently, means "accelerate at full throttle while grinning hysterically in the manner of a manic Indy 500 racer pumped up on CoCo Puffs and caffeine."

While in Quebec, be sure to visit Montreal, which is

the second-largest French-speaking city in the world after Paris. The Université de Montréal is the second-largest French-speaking university in the world after the Sorbonne. And so on. The centre of French culture on the continent, Montreal is a city of perpetual youth and long languid lunches. Ah, to be young again in Montreal! In Canada, the best life possible would be spent like this: you'd be nineteen in Montreal, thirty in Vancouver, fifty in Toronto, and sixty-five in Victoria. (Regina only enters into it after you've died, and then only if you've been very, very bad.)

The major holiday in Quebec is a pagan ritual honouring the Stay-Puff Marshmallow man. Events include craven images carved in ice, human sacrifices and kamikaze toboggan runs.

Note: There are actually *two* winter carnivals held in Quebec City: the tourist festival in the Upper Town, and the "real" festival in the Lower Town. The festival staged in the Upper Town is one of culture and tradition, featuring gaily coloured floats and quaint *habitant* customs. The festival in the Lower Town is about drinking.

The Lower Town is also the site of the annual "Miracle du Carnaval," a recurring miracle on a par with what happens at Lourdes. It involves getting drunk on *caribou* (which is, in essence, alcohol mixed with alcohol) and then passing out in a snowbank—only to wake up, hours later, with all of your digits still attached! *"C'est incroyable! C'est le miracle du carnaval!"*

The politics are nasty, the people are nice, the snow is deep, the signs are French, the laughter is genuine, and the shrugs are Gallic. Come to Quebec and lose yourself! Probably.

**ONTARIO: "Gaze upon Our Humble
Magnificence and Bow Down before Us!"**

Theme Song: "A place to stand [still during the regular traffic jams], a place to grow [uncontrollably], we call this land [which we have completely paved over] Ontari-airy-airy-o."

Location: Don't be a smart aleck. You know perfectly well where it is. You shouldn't have to ask.

Formal Name: The Centre of the Universe.

Pronounced: Ontario (or, to be more specific, "Toronto").

Main Hobby: Running the country. (Sorry: that was a typo. It should be *ruining* the country.)

Main Industries: Power, banking, politics, pissing off the West, deciding national elections, patting oneself on the back, and being at the forefront of each and every important technological innovation and business opportunity that other, less sophisticated provinces would be unable to attempt, let alone succeed at. In fact, they would probably fail. Miserably. The fools! *Bwahahahaha!*

Provincial Motto: "Celebrating over 100 Years of Narcissistic Self-Absorption."

First off, you don't hate Toronto. You just *think* you do. Toronto is a fine city. It is the *concept* of Toronto that you hate. And when we say Toronto, we mean of course "Ontario," the city having absorbed, bloblike, every other community within an 800-mile radius into the mega-city of "Greater Toronto."

Question: Is "Greater Toronto" a contradiction in terms? Explain.

Toronto (pronounced "T'ranna," or, in the West, #@!*&#!, or, in Quebec, "English Canada") is the great gravity well of Canadian society. Sooner or later, everybody ends up in Toronto, whether they like it or not.

Toronto is the largest city in Canada, and its main exports are insecurity and pride (usually unabashed—both the insecurity and the pride). It is precisely because they are so gnawingly insecure about their true status as a city that people in Toronto are inordinately proud of *everything,* especially if it involves being the biggest, longest or richest. They are proud of Yonge, which is in the *Guinness Book of World Records* as the longest street in the world (even though they included a large portion of Highway 11 when measuring it, the cheaters). And they are proud of their other world records as well. For example, the CN Tower, which is the world's tallest free-standing something-or-other. Or SkyDome, which is the world's most sophisticated retractable-roofed stadium. Torontonians also take pride in having the world's longest parking lot, which is what the Gardiner Expressway becomes every day during rush hour.

> *The Official Light Bulb Joke for Toronto, as created by Ian:* How many Torontonians does it take to change a light bulb?
>
> *Answer:* 2.5 million. One to actually change the bulb, the other 2,499,999 to walk around talking about what a world-class event that was.

There is more to Ontario than just Toronto. Not much more, but still. The province is, for example, home to

Niagara Falls, one of the great wonders of the world. Oscar Wilde, upon seeing the falls for the first time, remarked, with typical Shavian wit: "Wow. That's a lot of water. It's, like, falling and stuff." (This was, unfortunately, misquoted and misapplied over the years. "Second-biggest disappointment of married life blah blah blah a vast amount of unnecessary water blah blah blah the wonder would be if it didn't fall"—and so on, losing much of the brevity of the original.) Niagara Falls is the Honeymoon Capital of Canada, so you will *definitely* want to make sure the sheets have been changed when you check in.

Another Ontario destination, the cloyingly quaint town of Niagara-on-the-Lake, is home to the Shaw Festival, the only festival in the world honouring cable TV. And in Stratford, Ontario, they have a separate festival dedicated to the work of William "Bill" Shakespeare. A few minutes away from the Stratford Festival is the town of Shakespeare, which has absolutely no summer festival whatsoever. Nobody in Ontario considers this to be at all ironic. In fact, nobody in Ontario seems to understand irony. Which is sort of ironic, don't you think?

Northern Ontario, as a neglected colony of Toronto, naturally has a bit of an inferiority complex—and so they should. I mean, have you ever gone up there? Have you ever been to Sudbury? Good God, what a heathen, untamed wilderness. We're kidding, of course. No one would dream of selling Sudbury short. For one thing, to sell them short would require a buyer. (Still kidding!) The city of Sudbury, sometimes referred to as "the Pittsburgh of Canada—but lacking Pittsburgh's cultural cachet," is nevertheless home to one of Canada's best-known landmarks: the Giant

Nickel by the Side of the Highway (recently upstaged by the Giant Loonie Down the Road*). Sudbury also has an interactive science centre, French culture and, oh, so many other things. Make us an offer.

More towns and cities of note include North Bay, home to the province's former Premier for Life (the good citizens of North Bay had the sense to send Mike Harris as far away from them as possible); Thunder Bay, which is really two towns connected by a mall (and is right in the heart of the Canadian Shield—when you get to Thunder Bay you're either comfortingly close to Winnipeg but horribly far from Toronto, or horrifyingly close to Winnipeg but comfortably far from Toronto, take your pick); Dryden (where the town motto is "We don't breathe anything we can't see"); Kingston (which is actually located in Jamaica); Kenora (which is actually part of Manitoba); and Hamilton.

Ah, yes, Hamilton. The Steel City. "The Sudbury of southern Ontario." Famous for mill workers, Ti-Cats, outlaw bikers and—surprisingly, perhaps—a vibrant artistic community, Hamilton is actually not that bad. (Suggested tourist slogan: *"Hamilton: Not nearly as awful a place to visit as you've been led to believe."*) You can have a pleasant enough time in Hamilton, as long as you never, ever, ever mention Toronto. Seriously. You think Western Canadians dislike Hogtown? Try Hamiltonians. They *really* hate Toronto. Theirs is a profound, almost existential dislike. This is partly because of the close proximity of the two cities (familiarity breeding contempt and all that) and partly because, let's face it, it's just so easy to hate Toronto.

* Honest.

(After all, Toronto is a city where the mayor calls in the army whenever it snows—and the navy every time it rains, presumably.)

But the really odd thing about hating Toronto is that over 50% of the city's population wasn't even born in Canada, let alone Ontario. Of the remaining 50%, over two-thirds of them moved to Toronto from other areas of the country. That leaves, oh, probably only eleventeen percent or so that are *real* Torontonians. Born and bred. They're the ones causing all the problems. And when they tell you that they actually run the country, guess what? They mean it.

MANITOBA: "The Gateway to Saskatchewan"
Location: Right smack dab in the middle.
Shape: An upside-down Alberta. Very apt.
Main Industries: Wheat, wheat and more wheat.
Pet Peeve: People who are just passing through.
Favourite Hero: Louis Riel
Favourite Villain: Louis Riel
Official Mascot: Louis Riel
Provincial Motto: "Not quite the West, but not really the East either!"

Manitoba is rich in culture . . . if, when you say "culture," you mean "Ukrainian dance troupes." Manitoba exports more Ukrainian dance troupes than any other place on earth—and that includes Ukraine. Manitobans are also very proud of the fact that The Guess Who, Bachman-Turner Overdrive and Neil Young all come from Winnipeg. Mystifyingly, they also seem pleased as punch to claim Monty Hall, of *Let's Make a Deal* fame, as a native son.

People in Manitoba have had the good sense to assign appropriate names to their sporting teams. For example, the *Brandon Wheat Kings* of the WHL were named in recognition of the importance that Manitobans place on wheat, wheat farmers, wheat farms and all things wheat-related. *The Manitoba Moose* of the AHL were named in honour of the province's large and boisterous ungulate population. And the CFL *Blue Bombers* got their team name from an incident that occurred just prior to the First World War when a terrorist from the Balkans lingered too long on the corner of Winnipeg's Portage Avenue and Main Street. Unable to pry his frozen fingers off his Molotov cocktail in order to assassinate the visiting Archduke Ferdinand, the man later died of hypothermia. Nonetheless, he was responsible not only for providing the local football team with its unique name but also for confirming the perverse pride Winnipeggers take in the myth that Portage and Main is the coldest intersection in Canada. Actually, it isn't. There are other intersections where colder temperatures and harsher wind chills are occasionally recorded. They just happen to be in remote communities in the frozen Arctic that couldn't be bothered to name their streets.

Note: We're not trying to make fun of Manitoba or Winnipeg (especially considering that one of us* has in-laws in Winnipeg).

Freezing on street corners aside, there are lots of things to see and do in Manitoba, Land of a Thousand Friendly Lakes. You can watch polar bears meander down the main street of Churchill, you can observe Norwegians ambling

* That would be Ian.

down the main street of Gimli (but keep your eye peeled for aircraft running out of gas in the skies above), and you can even take a gander at all the non-Norwegians who, confusingly, live in the town of Norway House.

In Winnipeg, be sure to stop in at your neighbour-hood Salisbury House, where you can have a big nip with cheese—or maybe an order of deep-fried perogies*—and then put your feet up and spend some time watching the locals stagger painfully past outside as the bitter winds bite at them. This is most fun in summer.

SASKATCHEWAN: "Not as Flat as You'd Think!"
Location: Right where you left it.
Shape: Nothing but right angles.
Original Name: *Ksiskatchewanisipi*
Are you serious?: Yes.
Why did they change it?: Because they didn't want to have a name that was difficult to pronounce or spell.
You've got to be kidding: No.
Seasons: Variable.
Rain: Optional.
Capital City: Regina. You can't miss it, just go straight.
Provincial Motto: "Come to Saskatchewan and and enjoy the view!"

Note the use of singular in the above-mentioned motto. It's view, not views. There is only one view in Saskatchewan, and for the longest time, it looked like this:

---

* Actual item from the Salisbury House "Light Dinner" menu: *One dozen perogies. Includes sour cream.*

_____

Fortunately, the early settlers planted trees, so the view has greatly improved. It now looks like this:

_____^^_____

Saskatchewanites* take umbrage at the belief that their province is one long stretch of tedium punctated by the occasional grain elevator and/or stop sign. Saskatoon is a lively town and Regina is, well, Regina. And as Saskatchwooners are quick to point out, the Cypress Hills are actually the highest elevation between the Rockies and someplace way out east. Maybe in Quebec or something. This would be more impressive if anyone actually *lived* at Cypress Hills. They don't. They live in towns like this one.

_____MMMMMM____^^_____

While in Saskatchewan, make sure you visit the "Prairie Pimple"! Saskatoon was once awarded a national winter games, which naturally involved downhill skiing. Downhill skiing, as you may have guessed, requires a hill. Since it seemed unwise to ship everyone to the Cypress Hills and pray for snow, something drastic needed to be done. The solution? A giant mound of garbage was created and then covered with sod and named Blackstrap Mountain. Otherwise referred to as "the prairie pimple." (True story.) What's next, a Saskatchewan Surfin' Safari? Pearl diving in

* Saskatchewinians? Saskatchawaners?

Prince Albert? Beach volleyball in Bienfait? Ocean cruises in Esterhazy? Nothing is beyond the ability of these innovative and slightly loopy prairie folks.

There used to be a lot of buffalo in Saskatchewan, but they were hunted down and killed, something that is celebrated in Regina's fun-filled Buffalo Days festival. Regina itself was originally known as "Pile o' Bones" but they changed the name because, well, it was just too darn silly. (*See* Moose Jaw.)

In fairness to the people of Saskatchewan, who are often armed, we should note that the province does have a long and fascinating history involving gophers, dust storms, droughts, tornados, swarms of grasshoppers and—just for fun—the occasional armed uprising. Saskatchewan is also the birthplace and heartland of Canadian socialism, which is all the more ironic when you consider that it is right smack up against . . .

ALBERTA: "Back Up, Nice and Slow, and No One Gets Hurt."
Location: Left of centre (oddly enough).
Main Exports: Wealth and alienation.
Giant Ukrainian Easter Egg: Yes.
Giant Statue of a Sausage: Yes.
Giant Perogy: Yes.
Statue of King Kong: Yes.
UFO Landing Pad: Yes.
What, are they crazy?: And how!
Provincial Motto: "We have oil. We have money. We have guns. Don't piss us off."

Albertans are the angriest people in Canada. And why shouldn't they be angry? Just look at all the money and resources and land they have. It's enough to make *anyone* cranky.

Alberta pumps more cash into Confederation than any other province, and yet it has absolutely zip influence on setting the national agenda. Which is just as well, because if Albertans did have a say in setting the national agenda, every E.I.-dependent Maritimer east of Moncton would have been rounded up at gunpoint by now and sent to work camps in the interior. (Fort McMurray, an isolated tar sands outpost completely cut off from the rest of civilization, is inhabited entirely by homesick, ex-pat Newfoundlanders.)

Albertans believe in Western hospitality, but don't push your luck. This is a straight-talkin', straight-shootin' province (with the emphasis on *straight*). Albertans do not suffer fools gladly, which is why they have such an antagonistic relationship with the federal government.

The province of Alberta, and the city of Calgary in particular, have generated several populist political movements, including the Reform Party, the Alliance, the Reform Alliance, the Alliance Reform, the Reformed Alliance Reformers and, of course, the Let's Hunt Down Those Damn B.C. Tree-Huggers and Use 'Em for Target Practice Party.

Calgary, however, has grown tired of its right-wing "cowboy" image. It is, after all, a city that boasts the most highly educated population in Canada. (True.) So the people of Calgary have come up with a cunning plan to improve their image and dispel these out-of-date "Cowtown" stereotypes. They do this by holding an annual stampede jamboree in which everyone dresses up in cowboy hats and spurs and chews tobacco and shouts "yee-haw" and "woo-hoo" at random moments as though stricken with some sort of rustic backwoods Tourette's syndrome. The businesses—banks and law firms alike—decorate their lobbies with bales of hay and cowboy cartoons. And oh God, we wish we were making this up.* Sigh. The city of Edmonton, meanwhile, holds a Klondike Days festival every year to honour the fact that the Klondike gold rush happened somewhere else.

There are no rats in Alberta, except in the provincial legislature and West Edmonton Mall (*see* Mall rats, difficulty in exterminating.) The skies are big, the roses are wild, the music is country, the country is western, and the Rockies are right there. *Alberta: Disgruntled since 1905— and proud of it!*

BRITISH COLUMBIA: "Recycled, Free-range, Hand-woven— and All Organic!" (Rust is organic, right?)

Location: Somewhere between California and Alaska, appropriately enough.

Main Industries: Forestry, whaling, tourism.

Main Hobbies: Anti-forestry, anti-whaling, anti-tourism.

Main Export: Beef.

Main Import: Vegans.

Provincial Flower: Mildew.

Sunshine: Intermediate.

Long-term Forecast: Not so good.

Provincial Motto: "We don't think that's very funny."

Now, we're not saying the West Coast of Canada is a haven for spaced-out, looney-tune, New Age, wacked-out flakes, but it is a fact that at any given moment 70% of the popula-

---

* Will lives in Calgary, you see.

tion of B.C. is chained to a tree. And the remaining 40% is attempting to cut it down. (I know the numbers don't add up, but then, neither does B.C.) The Interior is filled with right-wing ranchers. The coast is filled with tossed salads and left-wing nutbars. The Island is filled with crotchety old retired folk. The Liberals are really conservatives, and the conservatives are really Socreds. Does any of this make sense?

It used to be that the one thing uniting Canadians, coast to coast to coast and regardless of their background or political leanings, was this: they all hated Toronto. Today, however, what most unites Canadians is a simmering dislike (read: envy) of Vancouver. This is why Toronto-centric newspapers (read: national media) have taken to publishing in-depth investigative reports on Vancouver with headlines like "A CITY IN DESPAIR! AMID THE NEEDLE-STREWN, JUNKIE-INFESTED, MEAN STREETS OF A FALLEN DREAM, VANCOUVERITES ASK, 'WHERE DID WE GO WRONG?'" (*Note:* The United Nations recently ranked Vancouver as the best city in the world in which to live. But what do they know?)

The official emblem of Vancouver is an umbrella turned inside out. With an activist chained to it. Drinking a latte. Vancouver: It's not just a city, it's a state of mind.

The capital of British Columbia is Victoria, a sun-dappled island outpost of Olde Englande, complete with double decker buses and afternoon tea—served with tofu burgers and soy milk. Victoria's municipal motto: "Snow? What is this thing you call snow?" Favourite pastime? Making crank calls. (That is, phoning up the other provinces in the middle of February to ask if the flowers are blooming where they are and then laughing and hanging up.) Victoria: Home of the newly wed, the nearly dead and the underfed. "Quick, get that senior to a White Spot!"

Lair of the Ogopogo and the place where the sun sets on the nation, B.C. is a land of Tai Chi and chai tea, where the trees are cedar, the condos are leaky, the coffee is Starbucks, the tie is dye, the poles are totem, the reviews are mixed and the stone-age neanderthal Sasquatch is real.

British Columbia: You can't beat it! Well, you could, but it probably wouldn't do any good.

YUKON: "There's Gold in Them Thar—Aw, What's the Use?"
Location: Look up, look waaay up . . .
Grizzled Old Prospectors Who Say Things Like "Con'sart it" and "Eureka!": No.
Teenagers Who Wear Nike T-shirts and Listen to Rap Music: Yes.
Storefronts in Dawson Meant to Resemble Brothels: Yes.
Actual Brothels: No.
Territorial Motto: "For the last time, we're not part of the United States. You're thinking of Alaska. We're right next door."
Use of "The" in Front of Yukon: Discouraged.
Relationship with the Rest of Canada: Generally strained.

Northerners tend to view southern Canadians (anyone who resides below the 60th parallel) in much the same way that Canadians view Americans. Meaning, they mistake our apathy for ignorance and think we're being condescending and mean-spirited whenever we show any sort of mild interest in what might possibly be going on up there. They think we're patronizing them or something. (Isn't that cute? They think we're patronizing them. That is *sooooo* cute.)

The main industries of "the" Yukon used to be gold mining and fur trapping. However, since the end of the gold rush and the demise of the fur trade (thank you so much, Brigitte Bardot), the main activities (you can't really call them industries) consist of A. working for the government, and B. staging gruelling week-long dog sled races. The latter is done in a futile attempt to encourage tourism. It ain't working. The really masochistic eco-tourists head for the Northwest Territories. Or Sudbury.

Robert W. Service wrote most of his poems while living in a cabin in Dawson City—and working for the government. Famous Canadian historian Pierre Berton also hails from Dawson City. He was born in the Yukon because his father had a job there—working for the government. Margot Kidder, mildly famous Canadian actor and notorious "free spirit," was born in Whitehorse. Guess what her parents did for a living?

So why even have a Yukon territory? It's a matter of national sovereignty, that's why. If the federal government ever abandoned the Yukon, Alaskans would move right in and turn the place into a rip-roaring success. They would eliminate the Yukon Quest—a week-long dog sled race—and the sub-par American version (the Iditarod) would finally achieve the prominence those Yanks have desired for so long. They'd probably also reopen the brothels and incorporate them into a giant theme park. A dirty Disneyland. And we don't want that to happen. Do we?

NORTHWEST TERRITORIES: "It's a Dry Cold."
Location: Top of the world, Ma!
Igloo-shaped Church: Yes.
Church-shaped Igloos: Oddly enough, yes.

Polar bear–shaped Licence Plates: Affirmative.

Main Industries: Copper mining, oil exploration, and preying on really dumb, misguided people who are willing to pay good money to travel all the way from Germany or Japan just to sit in a snowbank and freeze their nuts off on the slight chance they might get to sneak a peek at a polar bear or a musk ox (also known as "eco-tourism").

Motto of the Territorial Tourism Association: "Give us your money, you stupid, stupid people."

Ian and Will grew up in northern Alberta, near the NWT border, and family holidays inevitably involved mind-numbing car trips into the True North to gaze in awe at the skyline of Hay River (which consisted—this is true—of exactly one tall building) or to travel the magnificent gravel road leading up and over to Fort Smith ("Gateway to Wood Buffalo National Park!"). So you'll excuse us if we are less than thrilled about recommending the Northwest Territories as a fun-filled family getaway destination. Our memories are mainly of fending off hordes of mosquitoes while trying to outrun rutting bison.

The Inuit belong in the NWT. It's their home. Outsiders come in search of romance. Or something. Most live in Yellowknife. The rest are scattered around in remote villages and distant former fur-trading posts. They spend the long, lonely nights staring at the pictures coming in via their satellite dishes and thinking, "It *is* better in the Bahamas." But don't feel too sorry for them. Why? Because most of them have high-paying government jobs. There's this little thing called the "Northern Allowance," which is essentially a bribe the government pays to get people to work in the frozen wastelands. And why would the government go to all this trouble? Again, to protect Canada's "northern sovereignty" (*see* Yukon brothels, reopening of).

NUNAVUT: "Trees?"

Seasons: Two. Winter and Black Fly.

Mean Temperature: Yes. Even nasty sometimes.

Cultural History: Second-largest producer of authentic Eskimo art (after Taiwan).

Diet: Lard and bannock (with an occasional side of bacon).

Northern Lights: Yes.

Light Northerners: Very rare.

Territorial Motto: "A festival of utilidors!"

Nunavut is Canada's newest territory. Population: four. Government subsidies: $830 million gazillion—per day! And well worth every penny. Some have called Nunavut "the world's most expensive guilt trip," but that simply isn't true. It's less a territory than it is karma in action. Years of neglect and misuse finally bit Canada on the ass. You want to hold onto the arctic islands, largest archipelago in the world? Well, folks, there's a price to pay.

The Arctic has been called "Canada's Kalahari." Of course, unlike the Kalahari desert, which is bitterly and remorselessly hot, the Arctic is bitterly and remorselessly cold. Except for six days in summer. Well, actually, those six days *are* summer. That's when flesh-eating bugs the size of flying Volkswagen vans come out of hibernation looking for a snack. The Kalahari has ravenous packs of jackals. The North has bugs. Given a choice, we would go with the ravenous jackals.

Like the people of the Kalahari, the indigenous inhabitants of the Far North have historically been treated with an almost antagonistic disregard. And, as in the Kalahari, the government now pumps billions and billions of dollars into the region as a way of—okay, so it's not exactly like the Kalahari.

Note: We figure the odds are slim that any of our readers will ever actually get to Nunavut. So we could probably write just about anything we want and you'd believe us. Not that we would. We don't believe in taking advantage of people's trust.

Anyway. The best thing about Nunavut? The giant corkscrew licorice trees and the dancing winged narwhals. Like you're ever going to go.

CHAPTER 3 SUMMARY: WHAT YOU'VE LEARNED SO FAR

Rather than attempt to summarize the very important information contained within this chapter, we'll just say that we're awfully sorry we weren't able to name every interesting and/or annoying town in Canada. We were, of course, limited by considerations of space, time and interest (on our part). If you feel slighted or overlooked, simply send us a letter care of our publisher and we'll be pleased to think up something insulting to say about your hometown. If we *did* mention your hometown, and you *are* insulted by any of the comments we made and feel we were acting with reckless disregard for the feelings of the good people of your fine community, we'd like to say two things in our defence: A. we have been to every single place we talk about, and B. you're right.

4

LEARNING
THE LANGUAGE

. . . .

How to Talk

Like a Canadian

*T*YRE CENTER...

Well, that's just plain wrong, isn't it? As any true Canadian will tell you, both words are spelled incorrectly. It should be: TIRE CENTRE. Right?

Canadian English is a hodgepodge hybrid that operates according to its own eclectic rules, and Canadians just sort of make it up as they go along.

American: Tire Center · *British:* Tyre Centre
Canadian: One from Column A and one from Column B. Hence, the oddity of "Tire Centre."

Confused? Consider the following:

Canadians write cheques for their colour TVs. They turn off the tap, eat porridge, put jam on their toast and gas in their trucks, and munch potato chips as they relax on their chesterfields.

For those keeping score, the tally runs like this:

British English: cheque, colour, tap, porridge and jam. (In the U.S. it would be check, color, faucet, oatmeal and jelly.)

American English: TV, gas, truck and potato chips. (In Britain it would be telly, petrol, lorry and crisps.)

And that leaves the word "chesterfield," which belongs in neither list. A chesterfield is what Americans call a "couch" and Brits call a "sofa." Or is it the other way around? Not that it matters. Canadians use all three—couch, sofa and chesterfield—with equal aplomb.

IMPOSTER ALERT!

As a fledgling Canadian, you will have to be extra-vigilant. There are a lot of imposters out there. If you suspect that someone is falsely trying to pass themselves off as a Canadian, make the following statement—and then carefully note the reaction:

Last night, I cashed my pogey and went to buy a mickey of C.C. at the beer parlour, but my skidoo got stuck in the muskeg on my way back to the duplex. I was trying to deke out a deer, you see. Damn chinook, melted everything. And then a Mountie snuck up behind me in a ghost car and gave me an impaired. I was S.O.L., sitting there dressed only in my Stanfields and a toque at the time. And the Mountie, he's all chippy and everything, calling me a "shit disturber" and whatnot. What could I say, except, "Chimo!"

If the person you are talking to nods sympathetically, they're one of us. If, however, they stare at you with blank incomprehension, they are not a real Canadian. Have them reported to the authorities at once.

The passage cited above contains no fewer than *nineteen* different Canadianisms. In order:

pogey: E.I.(Employment Insurance). Money provided by the government for not working. Much like the salaries of members of the Canadian Senate, but smaller.

mickey: A small bottle of booze. (A Texas mickey, on the other hand, is a ridiculously *big* bottle of booze, which, despite the name, is still a Canadianism through and through.)

C.C.: Canadian Club, a brand of rye. Not to be confused with "hockey stick," another kind of Canadian club.

beer parlour: Like an ice cream parlour, but for Canadians.

skidoo: Self-propelled decapitation unit for teenagers.

muskeg: Boggy swampland. (Also: swampy bogland.)

duplex: A single building divided in half with two sets of inhabitants, each trying to pretend the other doesn't exist while at the same time managing to drive each other crazy; metaphor for Canada.

deke: Used as a verb, it means "to fool an opponent through skillful misdirection." As in, "Man, did he ever deke you outta your shorts." As a noun, it is used most often in exclamatory constructions, such as: "Whadda deke!" Meaning, "My, what an impressive display of physical dexterity employing misdirection and guile." (Do you see just how compact a good Canadianism can be?)

chinook: An unseasonably warm wind that comes over the Rockies and onto the plains, melting snowbanks in

Calgary but just missing Edmonton, much to the pleasure of Calgarians.

Mountie: Canadian icon, strong of jaw, red of coat, pure of heart. (*See also* Pepper spray, uses of.)

snuck: To have sneaked; to move, past tense, in a sneaky manner; non-restrictive extended semi-gerundial form of "did sneak." (We think.)

ghost car: An unmarked police car, easily identifiable by its inconspicuousness.

impaired: A charge of drunk driving. Used both as a noun and as an adjective (the alternate adjectival form of "impaired" being "pissed to the gills").

S.O.L.: Shit outta luck; in an unfortunate predicament.

Stanfields: Men's underwear, especially Grandpa-style, white cotton ones with a big elastic waistband and a large superfluous flap in the front.

toque: Canada's Official National Head Apparel, with about the same suave sex appeal as a pair of Stanfields.

chippy: Behaviour that is inappropriately aggressive; constantly looking for a reason to find offence; from "chip on one's shoulder." (*See* Western Canada.)

shit disturber: (*See* Quebec.) A troublemaker or provocateur. According to Katherine Barber, editor-in-chief of *The Canadian Oxford Dictionary,* "shit disturber" is a distinctly Canadian term. (Just remember that Western Canada is chippy and Quebec is a shit disturber, and you'll do fine.)

Chimo!: The last sound heard before a Canadian falls over.

So you can see the wide range of topics covered by Canadianisms, everything from drunk driving to men's underwear—philosophical terms and intellectual concepts being strangely absent.

Your next step, having mastered Canadian spelling and usage, is to tackle the single most important badge of citizenship yet devised. Master it, and you will be well on your way to becoming a true Canadian. Ladies and gentlemen, we give you the ejaculatory exclamation *"eh?"*.

"EH?": THE ULTIMATE EMBLEM OF CITIZENSHIP

First, a fable: The tribes of Gilead are at war with the Ephraimites. Gilead controls the mountain passes, and thousands of Ephraimites are trapped behind enemy lines. In desperation, a band of Ephraimites—indistinguishable in appearance from the Gileadites—attempts to get through. We join the story already in progress.

> When those Ephraimites which were escaped said, "Let me go over". . . the men of Gilead said unto them, "Art thou an Ephraimite?" If he said, "Nay," then said they unto him, "Say now Shibboleth." And he said "Sibboleth" for he could not frame to pronounce it right.
>
> Then they took him, and slew him at the passage of Jordan: and there fell at that time of the Ephraimites forty and two thousand.—*Judges 12:5–6*

Aside from the obvious theological lessons and the ethical questions that are raised ("What if it was just some poor Gileadite with a speech impediment?"), this biblical tale has given us a very useful term: *shibboleth,* meaning "a distinct word or pronunciation that sets one group apart from another."

In Canada, the national shibboleth is as elemental as the first letter in the alphabet, as ineffable as an autumn rain, as elusive as a summer sigh. In a word: *eh?*.

Eh? is what separates Canadians from the unwashed, envious hordes outside their national boundaries. (You know who you are.) *Eh?* is the secret password, the cross-Canada countersign, a two-letter, single-syllable symphony that takes years of diligent study to master. It must flow naturally into the sentence. It must never stand out, never call attention to itself—and yet must remain inextricably linked to the harmonial whole. It should trip melodiously off the tongue. "Howzit goin', eh?"

Canada's multilayered, contextual use of *eh?* is often compared to the American use of *huh?*. This is erroneous. Americans don't have what it takes to wield an *eh?*. That may sound harsh, but it is true. The authors of this book have a whole slew of thick-tongued, slack-jawed American cousins who have never mastered the intricacies of end consonants. Simple sentences like "That was priddy good, *eh?*" come out as one extended vowel movement: "Thaa wuh raal guh, *huh?*"

To make matters even worse, for one (blessedly brief) moment, Canadian comedians Rick Moranis and Dave Thomas, in their Canuck-caricature roles of Bob 'n' Doug McKenzie, were big hits south of the border. You may remember Bob 'n' Doug; they had a segment on SCTV called "Great White North," which mainly involved them sitting around in toques and parkas, drinking beer and saying things like "Take off, *eh?*" Many Canadians mistook this for a documentary.

Bob 'n' Doug were, however, inexplicably popular in the

United States, and so, for one (painfully long) summer, the authors of this book had to endure their visiting American cousins imitating Bob 'n' Doug in an apparent effort to blend in with the rustics. It didn't work. Americans simply cannot speak Canadian. Their *eh?*s always come out too nasally, too loud and too self-conscious. ("So, how is it going. . . AYE?" as opposed to "Howzit goin', *eh?*") If the U.S. and Canada ever go to war, this difference is going to come in very handy. "You wouldn't be a spy now, would'ja?" "Who ME? No way. . . AYE?" Sound of gunfire, followed by a dying gasp: *"Huuuhh?"*

This scenario is not as far-fetched as it sounds. According to an article by Harold B. Allen in *Canadian English: Origins and Structures* (this is a real author and a real article), the use of *eh?* "is so exclusively a Canadian feature that immigration officials use it as an identifying clue." Scary, eh? (Mind you, Allen doesn't make clear whether it is used by Canadian immigration officials to allow Canadians *in,* or by foreign immigration officials to keep Canadians *out.*)

Regardless, the use of this exclamation remains the clearest badge of Canadian citizenship, what the BBC called Canada's "national tic": the expressive, habitual, glorious *eh?*.

In it, one can find hints of the national character. *Eh?,* as you may have noticed, is *always* followed by a question mark, and thus, although it is essentially good-natured, it is also a bit insecure. It is an agreement looking to happen.

"It's cold out, eh?" "How about them Leafs, eh?" "Dialectical materialism was an inherently flawed conceptual model, eh?"

Advertisers and market researchers have long known the sly, subliminal appeal of a few well-placed *eh?*s. The three best-selling brand names of cigarettes in Canada? Export, *eh?* DuMarie, *eh?* and, of course, Craven, *eh?*—perhaps the single most aptly named cigarette ever. (As in: "Jeez, I'm all outta smokes. And I got this awful cravin', *eh?*")

In Canada, jazz musicians don't play "Take the A Train" but rather "Take the Train, eh?" Asked to spell "Canada," the average Canadian will unconsciously pronounce it thus: C, *eh?* N, *eh?* D, *eh?*. The Father of the Country? Sir John, *eh?*. . . And so on.

In conversations involving Alcoholics Anonymous, Canadians never know when to stop.

FIRST GUY:"Did'ja hear? Dave's in A.A., eh?"
SECOND GUY:"A.A.A.? What's that?"
FIRST GUY:"Not A.A.A., eh? A.A., eh?"
SECOND GUY:"*Eh?*"
FIRST GUY:"Not A! A.A., eh?"
SECOND GUY:"A.A.A.A., eh?"

. . . and so on, ad infinitum.

Further proof: We have before us a faded news clipping dated June 20, 1992, featuring a photograph of Air Canada pilots protesting Ottawa's delay in approving an air link to Tokyo. One protestor carries a placard reading: DESTINATION TOKYO! A good forceful slogan, that. But underneath it has been added, "Why not, *eh?*" This is classic Canadiana. A strong demand. A second thought, and then a tagged-on postscript to soften the blow.

Why not, eh? This is the quintessential Canadian question. It would be interesting to take a survey someday to determine how many Canadian marriage proposals contained that phrase—in both the question *and* the answer. ("Dale asked me to marry him, and I figgered, Why not, *eh?*")

"Why not, eh?" is a phrase at once plaintive and cajoling, and Canada is a nation of cajolers, the Land of the Hedged Bet. All that talk about the "national genius for compromise" is just a bunch of hooey. Canadians don't negotiate—they cajole. What was Confederation itself, if not the Cajoling of a Nation? No burning slogans. No guillotines. No oppressed masses yearning to be rich. Nope, the fathers of *our* nation sweet-talked their way into a union. "I mean, why not, eh?"

Eh? is symptomatic of the national reflex for ducking the question and avoiding the issues. It is a tendency so ingrained it has become second nature, even in statements that cannot possibly be disputed, such as "It's raining priddy hard, *eh?*" Which is to say: "It *looks* like it's raining priddy hard, but then, who am I to say? I mean, it's not like I'm an expert on rain or anything, right? I'm just saying it *seems* to be raining. And priddy hard too, eh?"

Now, at this point, you may feel that we have been giving too much attention to what is, after all, a single syllable. But consider the following actual statement by Thomas M. Paikeday, as quoted in the *Dictionary of Canadian Quotations*. "Utterances like 'eh?'," writes Paikeday, "are the relics of the animal cries from which human speech arose. As instinctive utterances, they have more or less the same meanings in most cultures. If one tribe of people is more addicted to one of these interjections, it is solely a matter of cultural identity."

Wow. All this time, what Canadians assumed was just a linguistic nervous tic is, in actuality, an "instinctive utterance," an animal cry.

Priddy cool, eh?

MAKING CONVERSATION WITH CANADIANS

To paraphrase Hobbes,* winter in Canada is brutish, nasty and long. Fortunately, most Canadians live indoors and rarely, if ever, have to cut open a caribou carcass and crawl inside for warmth. Except for the pre-dawn ritual of trying, mostly in vain, to get their cars to start, Canadians today have very little direct contact with winter. The days when you could go snowblind walking to the outhouse are, sadly, long gone.

But that doesn't make the eternal Canadian struggle against winter any less heroic! No sir. Even today, winter in Canada remains a Darwinian test of resolve and adaptability that favours only the very strongest. During the long winter months, Canadians fight to survive armed only with cable TV and copious amounts of carbohydrates to sustain them. Many of them become "stir crazy" with "cabin fever" and go stark raving "mad." These are the people who write letters to the editors of newspapers. (The first sign of trouble is an increased and arbitrary "use" of quotation marks.)

Sex, religion and politics are passé. In Canada, the real emotional energy and resulting passionate debate revolve around the weather (and when we say weather, we mean, of course, "winter"). Although Canadians try to minimize their contact with winter at any cost, they do love to talk about it. It is never cold enough for Canadians. Hence the

* Or possibly Carlyle.

question: "Cold enough for ya?"—the inevitable answer being "Are you kidding? It's only minus 50 out. This is nothing. When I was up in Timmins, it was minus 800 jillion, at least." Self-deluded regarding their endurance, self-congratulatory in their masochism, Canadians are a breed apart. When it comes to winter, they are legends in their own minds.

Americans: A Bunch of Copycats or What?

According to a recent report by a linguistics professor at the University of Toronto, Canadian and American dialects are becoming more and more similar. But it isn't simply a matter of Canadian English becoming Americanized. Far from it. The same report indicates that Canadian English, though subtle in its differences from that of Americans, is still robust and distinct. Sounds sort of like wine-tasting, no? "Subtle, yet robust."

In several instances, Canadian usage has even begun to infiltrate the U.S.—especially in the northern states. For years, Canadian English was the only standard English in the world where pairs of words like caught and cot, route and root, chock and chalk, not and naught, tot and taught were pronounced the same way. (In linguistic terms this is called "a Canadian low back vowel merger." In reality, it's called laziness.) The Americans are now beginning to adopt this pronunciation, meaning it will be even harder to pick the bastards off when it comes (inevitably) to war. The move towards a common North American dialect: natural linguistic evolution or nefarious American plot to destroy the Canadian way of life and pillage our land and culture?

So, to fully integrate into Canadian society, you will need to become familiar with the following vocabulary.

Chilly: Below zero with blowing wind and sleet

Nippy: Well below zero with gale-force winds, ten-foot-high snowbanks and roaming polar bears

Cold: Minus 40 with a wind-chill factor of at least 100 below (also known as "Jesus H. Christ, it's cold!")

Really cold: Exposed flesh freezes in ten minutes

Very cold: Exposed flesh freezes in five minutes

Damn cold: Two minutes

Really very damn cold: One minute

Freezing: Who needs all ten fingers anyway?

Too cold to go to the mall: Theoretical temperature used only in scientific hypotheses (like the infinity symbol, only more abstract)

Note: None of this applies to people living in Victoria, the bastards.

THE USES AND ABUSES OF JOUAL

So far we have been looking at Canadian English, but Canadian French is just as eccentric. Case in point: the Montreal street slang of *joual,* an east-end, blue-collar dialect. Unknown in France, *joual* is a completely home-grown phenomenon. Filled with street-beat and back-alley rhythms, it is Québécois Cockney, rough-and-tumble and looking for a fight. Pronounced "zhoo-AHL," the name comes from the local corruption of the word "horse," *cheval*—just as *j'suis* became "chus," *moi* became "moe," and *oui* became something resembling a quack. (That distinctive *"oui"* is to Quebec what "eh?" is to English Canada.)

The term *"joual"* was originally meant as an insult, and it still carries a pejorative sense—so be careful how you use it. For many people, *joual* was not so much a dialect as an affliction, something to be "cured." Playwright Michel Tremblay, a supporter and perpetrator of *joual,* prefers to call it *Québécois,* but even that, he admits, is a misnomer. It should really be called *Montréalais,* for that is what it is: an urban dialect.

In the small towns of the Gaspé region they speak another dialect entirely. In Quebec City, the French is more proper. And in the Lac-St-Jean area, the local "blue-berries" (as they are known) speak with an almost comical inflection. In Acadia, meanwhile, people also speak a separate dialect, one rife with archaic terms that have long since died out back in France. (Acadian French has its own sub-varieties as well, such as the raw-knuckled lumberjack dialect of les Brayons or the *Chiac* dialect of the coast—pronounced "shack," in reference to Shediac, New Brunswick, where they practically speak another language.)

Still, *joual* remains the best-known, or at least the most controversial, dialect of Canadian French. It is often criticized for the large number of anglicisms it contains, but *joual* doesn't merely copy English, it takes possession of it and makes it its own. The Quebec slang for car, *char,* is not a slurring of the English but in fact a corruption of the French *chariot.* In Quebec, any rust-ridden Trans Am can be considered a "chariot." And usually is.

And anyway, regular informal Canadian French is also full of anglicizations, even if it isn't always obvious. Some sentences are easy, like *j'ai drivé mon char downtown* or *je fait du shopping dans le weekend.* One can figure out *faire du shopping,* but how about *sur le slaille* ("on the sly") or *stepines?* Give up? It means panties, as in "step-ins."

The English verb "to call" is transformed into *caller* and then conjugated like a French word: *vous callez, nous callons,* etc. There are many examples: *luncher, se doper* (to do drugs) and *faker* (to pretend).

Faire une passe doesn't involve a football pass or a highway pass or a poker pass. So what does it mean? Hint: *faire du necking* usually follows *une passe.* What then becomes of that fine English verb "to French kiss"? In Quebec, they say—what else?—*frencher.*

What few realize, however, is that it cuts both ways. The Anglos in Montreal routinely use French words as though they were standard English terms. No one blinks if an English Montrealer says, "So I closed the light and took the auto-route to my friend's vernissage. We passed by the depanneur to buy some beer on the way."

How weird is that?

CHAPTER 4 SUMMARY: WHAT YOU'VE LEARNED SO FAR

The central lesson of this chapter? Canadians talk funny. If you want to sound like one, you must first master the ubiquitous eh? and the various terms used to describe "cold." Unfortunately, this could take a lifetime, so be prepared. Bring a lunch. Don't get discouraged, though. Practice makes perfect.

Here's a fun activity that will help you learn the language. Travel to different parts of the country. Go to as many bars and taverns as possible. Get drunk with the locals. Tell them you're there to teach them how to speak properly. Correct their grammar. Offer them constructive criticism about their regional dialect. This will please them to no end, and they will often decide to teach *you* a lesson as well. When you regain consciousness, immediately write down what you've learned.

The only place this approach doesn't work is in Quebec, where you'll have better luck if you adopt a snooty English accent and say things like "Oh, I just adored that Mordecai Richler" and "Ironic, don't you think, that English has become the *lingua franca* of the world?" That last one, in particular, is such a clever bit of intellectual japery that it's sure to go over gangbusters. You'll make a lot of new friends, and, more importantly, you'll learn a lot of new words. Some of which will even be printable.

5

LEISURE
ACTIVITIES

. . . .

How to Waste Time

Like a Canadian

*C*ANADA. Two solitudes. Not the English/French divide that occupies so much of our time and energy, but rather, the radically different ways Canadians characterize the amount of time they spend engaged in work-related activities vs. the amount of time they spend relaxing.

If you ask an average Canadian (and, really, is there such a thing as an average Canadian? Aren't we all unique and special in our own way?) about their job and/or career you will get one of two responses. You will also encounter two distinct personality types.

Type A Personality: "Work hard, play hard"

This type of person will be happy to regale you with endless stories of how stressed out and overworked they are, how their personal life is suffering, and how they really, really wish they could just give it all up and open a little bed and breakfast cum antique shop somewhere in cottage country. This person will respond to any inquiry regarding their employment with the unasked-for and unwanted information that they don't have a moment to spare. By gum, they're working so hard there's just not enough time in the day. This person approaches their leisure time with a type of grim fatalism, squeezing in workouts at the gym around visits to the local art gallery and maybe a quick trip to see their therapist.

Although they are commonly found throughout Canada, you're more likely to run into this type in Toronto and in certain areas of Vancouver. You must be very careful about how you approach them, as they are quite capable of wasting several hours of your day complaining about how hard they work. So be prepared. If you ask someone the simple question "So, howzit goin'?" and they launch into a litany of how little time they have to do anything, you must be prepared to take evasive action. Ask them to sign a petition outlawing the weekend, or, better yet, fake a heart attack. Remember, your time is valuable.

Typical Type A occupations (meaning, those containing people most likely to complain about being overworked and overbooked) include: stockbroker, attorney, Bay Street financier, breakfast cook at Husky House restaurants. And B&B owner/operator.

Type B Personality: *"Work? Hardly"*

The second type of person you will encounter is the one who answers the query "Working hard?" with the response "Hardly working." They will find this hilarious. Your best bet is to laugh knowingly, nod wisely, and fake another heart attack. Otherwise, you will have to listen to them complain about how that so-and-so at the next workstation does nothing but complain about how hard he works, even though he never seems to get anything done. You can run into this type anywhere, but they are most commonly found in the Maritimes—and in certain areas of Vancouver.

These people are capable of wasting large amounts of your time talking about abstract concepts like "quality of life" and the importance of "spending time with your family." Never mind the fact that the phrase "dysfunctional family" is a redundancy and that the more time you spend with your family, the stronger the urge to throttle them becomes. These people believe in the family as though it were some sort of Platonic ideal.

They also take great pride in unique leisure activities, like sitting on the board of the local alternative art gallery or organizing petition drives to have speed bumps and stop signs put in every driveway. Instead of therapists, they have "life-skill advisors." If pressed, they will tell you how much they're looking forward to retiring to cottage country, where they plan to continue their low-impact occupational aerobics by opening a little bed and breakfast. And maybe an antique store.

Typical Type B occupations (meaning, those containing people most likely to downplay the actual amount of effort they expend to earn a paycheque) include: museum curator, civil servant (someone who, despite the title, is neither civil nor sufficiently servile), fully tenured philosophy professor, wine steward at Husky House restaurants, and antique store owner/operator.

(There is a third type of Canadian, of course, who doesn't fall into either of the above categories. They're called the unemployed. You can find them in most parts of the country, and in most major cities. Just ask around. The unemployed may seem to have lots of time on their hands, but they actually have no leisure time per se, since they have to concentrate on things most of us take for granted, like hunting and gathering food and searching for shelter. And although they can be a bit annoying, you really don't have to worry about them taking up too much of your time, as their conversation will be limited to "Spare any change?" or "Hi there, I'm with the NDP, can I count on your support for our candidate in the next election?" In either case, the correct response is to give them a loonie or two, but remember not to make eye contact. And don't sign anything.)

It doesn't really matter whether you fall into Category A or Category B. In other words, you can complain about how little time you have, or boast about how little work you do, but the fact of the matter is we all put pretty well the same amount of effort into our chosen careers. Not too much, and not too little. Canadians work harder than people in some countries who work *longer* than we do (like the Japanese) and longer than people in some countries who work *harder* than we do (like the Swiss). And, when you look at the statistics comparing average hours-per-workweek and productivity, we fall right smack dab in the middle, between the slothful British and the overachieving Americans. If Canadians were porridge, Goldilocks would find us just right.

THE DAILY GRIND: A SCIENTIFIC
BREAKDOWN OF TIME WELL SPENT

So. Where does the time go? Glad you asked. Thanks to the hard work and diligence of the fine researchers and analysts at the Bureau of Unverifiable Statistics, we are pleased to present the following detailed breakdown of the average (there's that word again) Canadian working day. In a twenty-four-hour period, the average Canadian spends:

8.5 Hours Asleep

From our own estimates, this includes 5 hours and 10 minutes of actual sleep, 15 minutes of pillow adjustment, 20 minutes of lying still with your eyes closed while you wait to fall asleep, 25 minutes of tossing and turning, 30 minutes of longing for sleep, 40 minutes of thinking you will never get to sleep again, 55 minutes spent staring at the ceiling contemplating your own mortality, and 15 minutes (broken up into three convenient 5-minute periods) of fitful sleep squeezed in between repeated bashings of your clock when the snooze alarm goes off, waking you up to face another day of being alive. Hoo-ray.

1.5 Hours Commuting to Work

This figure is doubled if you live in Toronto—or if you work at home. It includes the 15 minutes you spend sitting on your bed trying to convince yourself that you should get up and get on with your day and not just go back to sleep and use your severance package to put a down payment on a small bed and breakfast in Grimsby. Or maybe Orillia. If you drive a vehicle, don't forget to deduct the time you spend using a credit card to scrape frost off the windshield. If you don't drive, remember: that same credit card can also be used as a handy shoe horn.

8 Hours at Work

Note: This means "8 hours *at* work," NOT "8 hours *working*." There is a big difference between the two. The 8 hours cited includes the 15 minutes you spend complaining to co-workers about A. the weather, B. the traffic, or C. how the weather *affected* the traffic during A. your morning car-pool commute, or B. your preferred method of public transportation, either A. buses, or B. trains, including A. subway cars, and B. monorails—and so on into infinite regress. It also includes the 30 minutes you spend playing sixteen games of solitaire on your office computer, the 45 minutes you spend playing one game of free cell, the half-hour you spend deleting unwanted e-mail jokes from your in-box, the hour and a half you spend on the Internet *looking* for dirty jokes, the half-hour you spend forwarding these alleged jokes to your colleagues, and the 45 minutes you spend on the phone with technical support when your computer performs an illegal function and needs to be serviced on-line. (Remember, if you work from home, all of these times will be doubled, except the time spent complaining to co-workers, which will be replaced by the time it takes you to give the cat her pill.)

You should also include the four 10-minute breaks that you take when you sneak outside to have a cigarette. If you don't smoke, this time can be constructively spent in A. a brief period of isometric exercise while seated at your desk, or B. the savage unwrapping and chewing of endless sticks of Nicorette.

Note: In Canada, the recent trend towards non-smoking work environments has led to a new form of social interaction, as the smokers, shunted outside like the pariahs they are, huddle together on the loading dock desperately inhaling the cool flavour of slow death and imminent lung disease. If you don't smoke, you should think about taking it up, since it will give you a chance to network with a wider range of co-workers. (Where else would you find the chief financial officer of a company turning to a mail-room clerk for support and encouragement?)

Many Canadians also leave work early in order to enjoy leisure time at a bar on their way home from work. That is, they go from sitting at work to sitting in a bar. The brief period of time spent looking for a place to sit in the bar constitutes the "exercise" portion of the day.

The 8-hour workday also consists of two 15-minute official coffee breaks and a euphemistically named lunch "hour." Add it all up, and that leaves a period of 2 hours, 35 minutes to actually get some work done. Now, don't you feel better?

1.5 Hours Eating

This does not include the work-related lunch "hour," but it does include the 5 minutes it takes to microwave a cup of last night's coffee and a stale bagel, and the additional 20 minutes it takes to consume them while commuting to work. *And don't forget!* Breakfast is the most important meal of the day. So make sure you eat it while in transit, preferably in a moving vehicle that backs up traffic for miles behind. That way your breakfast will think you're holding a parade in its honour, and it will know just how important it is. (Try to work a cell phone call or two and the application of eye shadow and/or the electric shaving of chin stubble into the equation for full effect.)

The time allotted for meals includes the 45 minutes you spend standing in front of your refrigerator at 8:00 P.M. trying to will something edible into existence before giving up and deciding to either heat up a microwavable entree (surely a contradiction in terms) or order in. The most efficient method would, of course, be to *order in* a microwavable entree.

45 Minutes Engaging in Personal Grooming

We admit that there is a slight statistical anomaly here, since this number can range widely depending on gender, age and whether you live in Newfoundland (less time required) or Quebec (more time—much more). We have chosen the median number. In the case of Will and Ian, total grooming time is reduced by 44 minutes, consisting as it does of sniffing one's armpits, shrugging, and then giving the teeth a quick once-over for any overt signs of spinach, fur and/or embedded winged insects. *Handy grooming tip from the Ferguson boys:* In lieu of showers, you can usually fool people with a liberal application of cologne. And, if you don't manage to fool them, they will at least stay the hell away, far out of smelling range. (Let's see the authors of *The Fabulous Girl's Guide to Decorum* top that!)

15 Minutes Having Sex

Note: The 15 minutes referred to here does not necessarily involve the participation of a partner.

All of this adds up to a grand total of 20½ hours to be deducted from the 24 hours available per day. That makes—let's see, carry the four, divide by the square root of seven—exactly 3½ hours left over to have some fun. Now, since Canadians spend the vast majority of each day doing stuff they have to do, what activities do they engage in when they get to do what they want to do?

THE BIG LIE (HEY, IF YOU'RE GONNA LIE, LIE BIG)

What do Canadians do with their leisure time? They watch television, like everyone else. Of course, in your encounters with Canadians you may find that they don't freely admit this. Right now, while you're reading this, the following conversation is taking place somewhere in Canada.

REGULAR PERSON: "Hey, did you watch that thing about those guys that do that stuff?"

UNMITIGATED SNOB (*or, for short, "a real John Ralston Saul"*): "Sorry?"*

NORMAL HUMAN BEING: "It was on television last night. These guys on this thing did this stuff. It was pretty wild."

SNOOTY DWEEB: "I'm sorry. But I don't watch television."

TYPICAL CANADIAN: "Really?"

---

* This is just one of the many variations of "I'm sorry," which we deal with in Chapter 16, "Twelve Ways to Say 'I'm Sorry.'" There are other examples in this book, and you'll have fun finding them all. Another funny, funny game would be to try to figure out which author wrote which section of the text. Here's a hint. Will is the suave, sexy, sophisticated one. Ian? He couldn't be bothered to read a footnote. He might not even know what footnotes are! He probably spent so much of his childhood breaking his brothers' Hot Wheels™ that he didn't even bother to study. Even the really cool Hot Wheel with the orange flames on the side.

PRETENTIOUS KNOB: "Except for the CBC, of course."

NEWLY INTIMIDATED AVERAGE PERSON: "Oh, of course. The CBC."

This is the Big Lie of Canadian television viewership. If everybody who claims to watch only the CBC were telling the truth, the cable companies would be out of business. And the other Canadian networks? CTV would be holding bake sales to pay for Lloyd Robertson's Grecian Formula, or whatever Dippity-do he uses to achieve that strange orange bouffant of his.

Seriously. Half the time Uncle Lloyd looks like a diseased alley cat has chosen his forehead as a good place to crawl up onto and die. It's really one of the most stunning public hairstyles ever, and it begs the question, "What's with Canadian news anchors and their 'do's?" Peter Mansbridge has a hairline that's receding faster than the ozone layer and the polar ice cap combined, Don Newman apparently found *his* hair in the Zeller's discount toupée bin, and Ian Hanomansing wears his in what can only be described as a mid-eighties mid-career William Shatner style. You know, back when Captain Kirk was pretending to be T.J. Hooker. And don't get us started on Wendy Mesley's Gumby do.

If CBC really had the market share that people at dinner parties claim, networks like Global would be so desperate for viewers they'd have to resort to rebroadcasting the most exploitive and degrading forms of "reality TV" they could possibly. . . hmmm. Wait a second.

The correct response when a Canadian tells you that they don't watch television (i.e., when they lie to you) is to smile and say, "But you are aware that it exists, right?

You do know that we have the technology to send pictures and sound over the air?" This will usually result in a quick change of subject, which, although welcome, will still prevent you from talking about whatever show you were watching the previous night. (Which is what Canadians talk about when they discuss "things." Things means "TV.") This is all fine and good, unless the person in question decides to tell you about how hard they've been working instead. Feigned heart attacks, anyone?

CANADIANS: THE INTELLECTUAL SIDE

Out of the 3½ hours of spare time Canadians have left over each day, they usually spend at least three hours in front of the television. Which still leaves plenty of time for intellectual pursuits. For example, doing the *Globe and Mail* crossword ("An eight-letter word, beginning with 'Fergus' and ending in 'son,' meaning 'jejune,' 'sophomoric' or 'self-referential'. . . hmmm"). Or reading the horoscope in the *National Post* ("Today will be a perfect day to deregulate something"). Or perhaps perusing the cutting-edge commentary on the Canadian condition, as explosively presented in *Maclean's*: "Whither the CBC?" A hard-hitting, exclusive investigative report by the people who brought you "Whither Canadian Cinema?" and "Whither Canadian History?"

Handy Guide to Reading Canadian Newspapers: Leisure at Its Best

Canada's largest newspapers are, not surprisingly, named after mighty planetary bodies: *The Star!, The Sun!, The Globe!, The Daily Planet!* All the better to reflect the weighty, earth-shaking news that bursts forth from Canada on a regular basis. (Sample headline: PREMIERS MEET TO DISCUSS PROPOSAL.)

By far the best, most excellentest newspapers in Canada are those of the "plucky" (and by plucky, we mean "struggling financially") *Sun* newspaper chain. The various *Sun*s routinely win awards for best investigative paragraph at the annual newspaper awards ceremony.

But the *Sun* newspapers' greatest claim to fame are their wholesome and pleasantly airbrushed Sunshine Girls—which are sort of Canada's answer to Britain's page three girls. Except that A. Canada's Sunshine Girls are not topless, and B. they are not on page three. Or page two. Or even in the index. Meaning, you have to flip through the entire goddamn paper before you ever find them. Not that we look.

> "Fleecy, 19, enjoys long walks in the park with that special someone, horseback riding, tennis, pottery, poetry, and jumping out of airplanes with carefree abandon. She plans to be a marine biologist. Her life is more exciting than yours could ever be, and she would never, never, never go out on a date with someone like you. So there."

Oh yes, there is also apparently a Sunshine Boy, whose photo is usually clipped from a Sears catalogue and then pasted in beside the horoscopes and Ann Landers in order to appease the tens of women who read the *Sun*.

As for understanding media (which would be an excellent title for a book, don't you think?), you may find it helpful if you try to imagine how each of Canada's national newspapers might have covered a well-known historical event. Like, say, the discovery of fire. Here's how the headlines would have run:

Globe and Mail: "*Homo Erectus* may have found secret to keeping caves warm at night. Safety concerns grow"

National Post: "Liberals accused of hiding secret of warmth from other cave dwellers"

Sun: "IT BURNS! IT BURNS!"

Or, for example, the 1912 sinking of the *Titanic*:

Globe and Mail: "Luxury liner allegedly hits iceberg; many lives may have been saved by quick action of crew"

National Post: "Liberal cutbacks to shipping industry cost lives as hundreds die in Atlantic tragedy"

Sun: "WET T-SHIRT CONTEST!"

You can perform this exercise with contemporary events as well. Next time something happens, try to guess what the headline in each of the three papers will be the next day.

Helpful hint: The *Sun* has a hockey game on every second cover, so all you have to know is, Did the hometown team win? ("WE'RE GOING TO THE CUP!!") or lose? ("FIRE THE COACH, FOR THE LOVE OF GOD FIRE THE COACH"). The *Post* runs a Christie Blatchford column every second day, so something like "Shocking Disgrace!" or "Man, Am I Steamed" is a good guess for the headline game. As for the *Globe,* whatever the story is, it's going to be depressing.

You can count on it. The *Globe and Mail* will always find a way to put a pessimistic, wet-blanket spin on things. If cancer were cured tomorrow, the *Globe* headline would read: "Chemotherapy Clinics Facing Bankruptcy."

The *Globe and Mail* is like your dad. It calls you into the den after supper and tells you that it is greatly disappointed in you.

The *National Post* is like an uncle who takes you out for a beer—and then tells you that he is greatly disappointed in you.

WEEKEND WARRIORS

Canadians do a bit more relaxing on the weekends. That's when they go out to places with names like Colonel Hooter McNasty's Southern U.S. Alabama-Style Smoke-House

Odd but True

In spite of the fact that they can't spell worth a damn (*see* Toronto Maple Leafs, spelling of), Canadians regularly take top place in the world of Scrabble. To quote John Chew, past director of the Toronto Scrabble Club, "the world's largest and oldest," Canadians are—get ready for a great quote—"a nation of really good Scrabble players." Quick! What's a ten-letter word for "Who cares?" We're kidding, of course. Scrabble is a fine game, though not as engaging as Trivial Pursuit, a board game invented in Canada wherein participants sit around in a circle and ask each other pointless questions for a piece of pie. (Sample question: "Which city boasts the world's largest and oldest Scrabble association?")

Roaster & Goodtimes Emporium Bar & Grill. There is no need to feel guilty if you've recently patronized such an establishment, since most of the popular watering holes in Canada are actually owned by one giant, all-powerful, all-Canadian organization named CARA (which stands for "Canadian Association of Restaurants Association" or something). They also provide cafeteria cuisine and almost all of the airline food served domestically. And no, we're not making this up.

Canadians will, on occasion, spend a Friday or Saturday evening attending highly refined cultural activities at a museum or an art gallery. Or perhaps a symposium on the future of the CBC. Hosted by John Ralston Saul. But mainly they drink beer. And worry.

That's what Canadians do best. Worry. And what do they worry about? Oh, the usual stuff. That they're drinking too much. That they're putting on weight. Or that they're watching too much TV and not enough CBC: "Hey, look! Next on Fox: 'When Good Pets Go Bad!' Caught on tape." Time flies when you're having fun.

CHAPTER 5 SUMMARY: WHAT YOU'VE LEARNED SO FAR

Canadians fall into two categories. Some live for the weekend, some live for their work. Lots of them hate their jobs, some of them like their jobs, and a handful either have no job or, like the authors of this fine book, are lucky enough to do something that takes so little energy they are able to spend lots of time goofing off and going out for coffee and doughnuts. When Canadians have a little spare time, they don't spend it reading great works of literature or pursuing serious cultural activities. Mainly they hang out in bars and/or watch the boob tube. You can follow that basic approach, or you can go one better and, as a true Canadian, attempt to Do Good by becoming a volunteer. Try joining a local recreational board or one of the many Royal Commissions or Government Fact-Finding Committees that are floating around (see Chapter 14).

Even better, why not join Canada's broadcasting watchdog, the CRTC? That way, you could combine the various Canadian leisure activities into one: watching television, Doing Good, having no real effect and worrying.

6

SPORTS AND/OR RECREATION

. . . .

How to Watch

TV *Like a Canadian*

*O*NE OF the most important aspects of assimilating into a particular culture is getting interested in the national sporting obsession. In some countries, this is easy. Just moved to Japan? Become fascinated with sumo wrestling, particularly if there's a local boy to cheer for. "In this corner, Futoi Kujira: The Endangered Whale!" Going to the United Kingdom for an extended stay? You can't go wrong getting caught up in the continuous monotony that is soccer. Sure, they call it football, but it's really soccer, and, yes, the game is so gawd-awful dull and slow-paced that the fans occasionally engage in desperate attempts to wake up the crowd and perk up the ambiance. The authorities call it hooliganism, which is slightly misleading. They might as well call it "rascal-itis." It's really a full-blown riot. You'll find as a newcomer that it's easy to participate—indeed, that it's almost impossible not to—so take along a few uneven paving stones, stolen lawn darts and other projectiles and have a good time. You'll look as English as the next guy (although he's probably Irish, since they produce the world's best hooligans). The point is to get involved. You'll feel more at home, and people will treat you like a local. It's all about being comfortable in your surroundings.

When you're trying to fit in through a chosen sport, however, Canada presents a problem. It used to be easy. All you had to do was develop a love of hockey and root for the Montreal Canadiens and hate the Toronto Maple Leafs. Unless you lived in Toronto: then you were supposed to root for the Maple Leafs. The latter was usually done by repeating the chant "Wait 'til next year!" over and over until you actually started to believe it might come true. (This is the same way the Canadian Alliance concludes its national conventions.)

Unfortunately, there are now a lot fewer hockey teams in Canada than there used to be. There are also a lot fewer Canadians playing hockey than ever before. Which is a shame, because Canada invented the game, developed the game, refined the game and gave the game to the world. The world took the game, saw that it was good, and they ain't giving it back.

WISTFUL NOSTALGIA, CANADIAN STYLE
(ALSO KNOWN AS "HOCKEY")

Hockey matters to Canadians. Canadians care *deeply*. Anaheim vs. Nashville. San Jose vs. Phoenix. Who will win? Who will lose? Who could possibly care one way or another? Canadians, that's who. The National Hockey League is expanding everywhere except in Canada— where the fans and the players and the history are. Why? Well, it's certainly not because the NHL is run by a bunch of greedy money-toadying slugs. So there must be some other reason.

Here are the *Canadian* hockey teams. These are the ones you will need to know if you wish to take part in Canada's fast-paced guessing game of "Who will be eliminated from the play-offs first?"

Ottawa Senators: Team motto: *"Petulant Russian superstars are only the beginning!"* The Senators were named in honour of Canada's dynamic Upper House, whose members are, of course, renowned for their athletic prowess and energetic bursts of speed.

Toronto Maple Leafs: Team motto: *"Winning isn't everything!"* The Leafs are sometimes erroneously referred to as the "Maple Laffs," but that would suggest a certain entertainment value. Famous for *not quite* winning.

Montreal Canadiens: Team motto: *"A riotous time was had by all!"* The Canadiens are now owned by Americans. Which is oddly appropriate, somehow. *Note:* Any resemblance between the current Canadiens and *les Habs* of yesteryear is purely coincidental.

Quebec Nordi—no, wait, they're gone.

Winnipeg Je—no, they're gone too.

Edmonton Oilers: Team motto: *"We used to be really, really good! Honest."* Big hair, Jordache jeans and a winning team in Edmonton. Ah, yes, the eighties.

The team formerly known as the Vancouver Canucks (the team name was deemed offensive and has now been changed to the Vancouver Gender-Neutral Ethnically Inclusive Peoples): Team motto: *"Hey, it could be worse. We could be an NBA franchise!"*

Oh yes, there is also apparently a team in Calgary, but we haven't seen evidence of this for a long, long time. (Actual headline: "CALGARY REGAINS LAST PLACE!")

Is it any wonder that *Hockey Night in Canada,* once a ratings juggernaut, is now regularly bested by reruns of *The Beachcombers* on the Aboriginal Peoples Television Network? (APTN is one of Canada's new cable channels. They specialize in shows by and of interest to the First Nations. Reruns of *The Beachcombers* qualify because of the fine work done by Native actor Pat John in the very demanding role of Jesse Jim, the Indian sidekick. As we see it, there are only two problems with APTN. First of all, it's so far up the cable ladder you can give yourself a repetitive strain injury trying to click your way to it. Second of all, almost every time you tune in, somebody—we swear to God—is gutting an animal. Try it tonight. Go to APTN and odds are the first images you encounter will be the inevitable documentary footage of a caribou being gutted out. Or a moose. Or a deer. Although, once in a while, just to keep things interesting, they will field-dress a salmon instead. "We're now slicing open the fish's belly. . .")

And hey, you're still better off discussing salmon-gutting than you are trying to engage Canadians in fun-filled hockey talk. In Edmonton, in Calgary and, saddest of all, in Montreal, the entire topic of hockey is best avoided—unless you want to find yourself trapped in a melancholy sports bar listening to innumerable depressing conversations about the Future of the Game. Or, even worse, the Good Ol' Days When the Game Seemed to Have a Future.

And what about Vancouver? Well, since there is no empirical evidence that the local citizens are even *aware* that there is a hockey team in town, any attempts to engage in "sports chat" will likely be met with blank stares and incoherent mumbling. Don't be alarmed. They're not being rude. That's just the way people communicate on the Left Coast: with blank stares and incoherent mumbling. The beauty of their surroundings and their collective love of the environment cause them to be constantly awed by the effulgence of nature. Either that, or they're stoned (see Chapter 3).

A CUP FULL OF GREY

If hockey is no longer available as a general cultural touch-stone and sports panacea, what's left? Well, there is always the exciting Canadian Football League, consisting of eight teams, at least three of which are required to have the same name. "This just in! A late-breaking score from the gridiron. It's Roughriders 17, Rough Riders 11 in a classic battle of—no, wait. That should be *Rough Riders 17* and *Roughriders 11*. Sorry!" (This does come in handy for welshing on bets, though. "Rough Riders?? No, no, no. I said *Roughriders!*")

Football came to Canada via Britain, as "rugby." Canadians, with their legendary love of blood and spectacle (*see also* Hockey; Lacrosse; Question Period), were smitten, and "rugby-football" quickly became popular as a way for Canadians to brutalize each other during the hockey off-season. Canadians, in turn, introduced rugby to the States, and the game evolved into the football of today, with slight differences on either side of the border.

Alas, the glory days of Canadian football are long gone, and any social encounter you have regarding football in Canada will be with either A. someone who wants to convince you that their local town really, really, really deserves an American NFL franchise so it can become the truly, truly, truly world-class city they know in their hearts it already is (these same people will sometimes substitute the word "Olympics" for NFL), or b. someone who wants to bore your ears off with talk of how the Canadian game is superior in all ways to the American version. "Three downs, not four, eh? I mean, who couldn't move a freaking football ten freaking yards in four freaking plays? Eh? And our field is wider, and our balls is bigger, and our grass is bouncier and we don't have any fruity fair-catch rule" and blah, blah, blah.

The difference between U.S. and Canadian football lies largely in the glamour and PR factors. (Compare SUPER BOWL!! with Grey Cup.) But what really makes the Canadian game different from the American one are the absolutely appalling field conditions the players and fans have to endure in Canada. This is what you get for trying to play outdoor sports amid tundra and permafrost.

- There was the Mud Bowl of 1950, when the field became such a quagmire that the quarterbacks were forced to tape thumbtacks to their fingertips in order to handle the muck-caked ball.
- And then there was the infamous Fog Bowl of 1962, when the fog rolled in like pea soup and the teams essentially ended up playing a full-contact version of Blind Man's Bluff.
- And let's not forget the Ice Bowl of 1977, in which field conditions deteriorated to the point where a hockey game almost broke out. The winning team secretly

used a gun to punch industrial-strength staples into the soles of their shoes.

All true. Thumbtacks on fingers and staples in shoes? Must be Canadian football. Mud, fog, ice. What's next? The Plague of Locusts and Death of All First-born Males Game? For a while the CFL was toying with the slogan "Canadian Football: Come and watch the biblical prophecies unfold," but they decided it was a little too negative. And accurate.

Want to know the weirdest thing? The Grey Cup final is still the single most-watched televised sporting event in Canada—including the Super Bowl and the Olympics. Why? Because Canadians are walking grab bags of contradictions and eccentricities, that's why. Why would you watch a Roughriders vs. Rough Riders final being played in Hamilton and broadcast elsewhere? Sheerly out of a sense of duty and patriotism, is our guess. Because, let's face it, in Canada patriotism always involves a certain amount of masochism and fatalistic disappointment. Like in 1995 when, through a fluke of expansion, the Canadian Football League championship was won by a team in . . . Baltimore. Now, last time we checked, Baltimore was *not* part of Canada. But we could be wrong. After all, they had a CFL franchise, right?

WHAT ABOUT BASKETBALL?

Well, what about it? True, it was invented by a Canadian, one James Naismith, who was working at a YMCA in Massachusetts at the time. Naismith developed an indoor sport that would encourage healthy competition and provide a "brisk and vigorous work-out, with constructive team play." He hung peach baskets up at opposite ends of a gymnasium and used a soccer ball for passing. The game sped up considerably when someone thought to cut a hole in the bottom of the basket. (A similar advance had already greatly improved outhouse technology.)

Naismith's game bore little relation to today's run-and-gun, fast-paced, trash-talking, drug-taking, plea-bargaining NBA version. So much for healthy competition. So much for "constructive team play." Still, basketball is, in origins at least, a Canadian sport. It was developed by a Canadian, and then given to the world. You may have noticed a pattern here.

THREE-LEGGED SYNCHRONIZED BADMINTON

So, if not hockey, football or basketball, then what? Is there *any* one sport that truly unites Canadians? Is there any one sport that represents all that is good and pure in the land?

Canadians seem to excel at a handful of relatively obscure sporting events. Take synchronized swimming. Please. For the love of God, take it away! With all due respect to Carolyn Waldo, the fact that Canada once ruled the world of synchronized swimming doesn't exactly make our hearts swell with patriotic pride. And who came up with that sport in the first place? You can just imagine the planning session. "Well, it's sort of like swimming, but with music. It's kind of like the RCMP Musical Ride, only there aren't any horses, and everybody wears colour-coordinated nose plugs."

Canadians have a tradition of doing well in sports that have just been introduced. Ross Rebagliati won the first-ever gold medal in snowboarding, which is a very popular activity amongst the dope-smoking slackers in the mountains of British Columbia. It isn't really a sport, it's a distraction from the munchies. It's the wintertime equivalent of Ultimate Frisbee. In fact, Ross would have set a new record if he hadn't stopped halfway down to fire up a doobie and chill out awhile. Many downhill snowboarders don't even finish the run.

A lot of the so-called international sports that get trotted out every couple of years at the Olympics or the Commonwealth Games are just a tad weird. For example, badminton. Badminton is really only played in two places: China . . . and family picnics. We say why not agitate to get Lawn Darts™ and the three-legged race recognized by international sporting organizations as well.

GROWTHFULLNESS—ON ICE!

Canadians used to be major contenders in figure skating, but lately our bejewelled, rhinestoned, heavily made-up athletes (and, let's be honest, the women are almost as bad) have begun to, how to put this nicely, fall flat on their asses whenever the pressure of international competition becomes too intense. Which, lately, is every single friggin' time.

"My name is Bruce and I am . . ."—*splat!*

"Say, Bruce, that must have been a big disappointment. Anything you want to say to your legions of disgruntled fans back home?"

"Well, I tried really, really hard. I may not have come home with a medal. In fact, I may have fallen down so many times that they didn't need to bring out the Zamboni to resurface the ice, but overall I feel really good about the few things that I managed to do right, and I feel that this was an experience of great growthfullness."

That's right, *growthfullness*. This is the sort of speech that most figure skaters are taught before puberty. Gracious in defeat, surprised in victory. It's the Canadian way. "Thank you!" *Splat*. Watching Skate Canada, we saw more pale flesh hit the ice than the last time we watched them yank out a seal's viscera on APTN.

Synchronized swimming, figure skating, balloon animal twisting: these are Olympic events? Now, some people (and when we say "some people," we mean "you") may feel that Canada's medal count at the Olympics leaves something to be desired. But what some people don't realize is that Canada has actually been boycotting the Olympics for the last fifty years. It's just that no one has noticed.

By now, you may well be pulling your hair out by the handful, with tears welling in your eyes, desperation and dismay creeping into your voice. Without hockey or skating or swimming, what could possibly be left? What sport defines Canadian dreams and aspirations? Which athletic endeavour binds the country together like no other?

Two words: Televised curling.

CURLING: THE ULTIMATE CANADIAN SPORT

Canadians invented it (maybe), developed it (certainly) and refined it (the shot clock and the drunken bonspiel), and Canadians are the best in the world at it. Forget hockey. Curling is the answer. Curling is the cure. Curling *is* Canada!

And what is curling, exactly? It is a sport of great skill in which players compete to see who can drink the most and still stand on ice. Even better, it is a completely democratic undertaking. Anyone can play, regardless of physique, ability or sheer slothfulness. In what other sport can you drink beer and smoke while playing the game? Even bowlers have to occasionally put down their glass of beer and butt out their cigarette in order to participate. Curlers do not. In fact, curling is the only sport in the world *where you can win while you are taking a leak*. True story. The 2000 championship was won while the team captain was in the can. Seriously. So don't say curling isn't heroic.

And exciting? Whoo-boy. It's a game of inches. It's psychologically compelling. Imagine a chess game played on ice, with non-stop moments of excitement. Or moments of great inertia, broken intermittently with some action, or. . . well, okay, it's basically the same game as shuffleboard. Only on ice. If you aren't familiar with shuffleboard, it's that game you sometimes see in Canadian bars and taverns where you slide little disks back and forth on a surface that's occasionally sprinkled with Parmesan cheese. Closest disk to the centre gets a point. Same thing with curling, only on a larger scale.

Here's a brief glossary to help you understand the finer intricacies of the sport:

Beer: Absolutely essential. You can, in a pinch, curl without rocks or ice or a broom. But not without beer.

Sheet: The most important word to know if you want to sound like a truly knowledgeable fan. It refers both to the ice surface and to the condition of most players (sheets per wind: three).

End: Unlike football, where you would ask "Which half is it?", or hockey, where the question would be "Which period are we in?", or soccer, where you might inquire "Are they going to score a goal at some point before the next vernal equinox?", in curling you merely ask "Which end?" or, to really fit in, "Which end, eh?" Then you go and get another beer. There are ten ends in a typical curling game, but you don't have to know this. One team usually concedes around the sixth or seventh end, once a mathematical impossibility has been established regarding victory. If George Bush had been a curler, Al Gore would be president today.

Rock: These are huge polished slabs of granite, which the players take turns "throwing." Except they don't. Throw them, that is. (Even though that would make the game much more exciting. "He's getting ready to throw it . . . Run for your lives!") The players also used to swing the rock out behind them in a dramatic fashion before sliding it down the ice. This was done in the belief that the movement would increase the speed of the stone. Then someone discovered elementary physics, and they don't do that any more, eliminating one of the last vestiges of athleticism required by the game. Now players just sort of shove the rock away from themselves without exerting any real effort. That is, they have figured out how to make curling even *lazier* than it already was. Another triumph of Canadian innovation.

Sweep: This is what two members of the team do when a third member of the team throws a rock. (Except that they don't. Throw it, that is. See above.) Sweeping is supposed to heat up the ice, thereby accelerating the inside velocity of the rock's outward trajectory, thus enabling the fourth member of the team to yell HAAARRD! HARDHARDHARD!! This exhortation is followed by the anticlimactic sound of the brooms (i.e., *ikki-ikki-ikki-ikki*). Curling brooms used to be much cooler than they are now. The straw ones would go *whackatta-whackatta-whackatta,* and these, in turn, were replaced by giant foamies that looked like large blue tongues and which were used more for volume than technique, providing a reverberating BAMM-BAMM-BAMM-BAMM. It was very macho. Within the context of curling, that is. But not any more. Now all we have is the emasculated little ikki-ikki-ikki of modern curling sound effects. A sad day indeed.

Out-turn: When letting go of a rock, to release the handle of the rock with a slight twist to the left, to ensure it spirals as it travels down the ice. Used for accuracy.

In-turn: Same as above, except you make a right turn. (Illegal in Quebec if the light is red.)

U-turn: This, however, is perfectly legal in Quebec.

Weight: The force a rock carries. Also applies to the physical condition of the players.

Take-out: It's usually a good idea to stop on the way to the rink and pick up some doughnuts and maybe a couple of burgers to go.

Guard: The guy who keeps an eye on the case of beer when his team is on the ice.

Button: The first item on a uniform to pop off when curlers bend over to pick up their rock.

Bonspiel: A word meaning "tournament" or "big drunk." Trophies are often given out. Or prizes. In some bonspiels the prize is a bottle of Canadian whisky, although, let's face it, with the amount of drinking that goes on during an average bonspiel, both on and off the ice, providing more booze as a prize definitely falls into the category of redundancy.

Brier: Like a bonspiel, only televised, and the players usually don't do any drinking until after the game. This used to be the Macdonald Brier, sponsored by the tobacco company that makes Export A cigarettes, but the company quickly figured out that with the extensive smoking that goes on during an average game, they didn't need to waste any more money on advertising. The event is now sponsored by a cell phone company and is called the Nokia Brier. Which is to say, the sport of curling has exchanged the sponsorship of one form of public nuisance for another. (You'll notice our restraint in not making a comment about simply replacing one form of cancer with another.)

Note: The Brier is the national championship for all-male teams. The female championship is called the Scott Tournament of Hearts. It used to be sponsored by the makers of Export A as well, and was called the MacDonald "Lassie." Instead of prizes, the women curlers would get a nice, patronizing pat on the head. Ah, those were the days.

Hec: Not to be confused with *hack,* the small rubber foothold players use when they "throw" their rocks. Hec is the one and only Hector Gervais, from St. Albert, Alberta. He was one of the greatest curlers of all time, winning both the Canadian championship and the world's. He was also, how shall we put this, a rather large man. Not only was he unable to tie his shoes, he couldn't even see his feet. Hec Gervais played the game with a smouldering Export A permanently affixed to his lip, a cold can of Molson in his left hand and a steely glint in his eyes. He weighed 415 pounds at the peak of his game, and if they ever decide to turn his life into a musical, Canadian tenor Ben Heppner, who has a classic curler's physique, would be perfect for the part. Although he might have to gain a little weight.

If there was a Canadian Curling Hall of Fame, and we're pretty sure there isn't, Hec Gervais would be the first inductee, a man of gargantuan appetites, huge victories and heroic jowls. If Hec Gervais had been a hockey player, he would have been Wayne Gretzky (only fatter). If he had been a basketball player, he would have been Vince Carter (only fatter). If he had been a baseball player, he would have been Babe Ruth. Only fatter!

We're not knocking Hec, though. If you don't think it requires tremendous athleticism to walk on ice when you're half-cut, well then, you've never tried it yourself.

So: if you want to become a serious Canadian athlete, grab that beer, light that cigarette and "throw" that stone. Just remember to bend from the knees. Thank you.

CHAPTER 6 SUMMARY: WHAT YOU'VE LEARNED SO FAR

Canadians used to be real good at hockey. Now they suck. There was once a Canadian Football League that was real good. Now it sucks. Canadians are good at sports that nobody cares about and they suck at sports that matter. Also, curlers are easy to make fun of. Because they're curlers. And that's pretty well all you need to know about Chapter 6.

However, as always, we do have some advice for you that will help you fit in whenever a sporting event of any kind is under discussion. Trust us. This will work every time. No matter which sport is being discussed, all you have to do is squint your eyes, grunt deeply, wave a hand dismissively and say, "Aw, it ain't the game it used to be." This will get a chorus of affirmative grunts from everybody else, and then you can follow up with, "Sometimes, I can hardly bring myself to watch." Again, no matter what sport everybody's been talking about—hockey, football, lawn darts—this comment is sure to win sympathy and nodded agreement. But don't push your luck. If anybody tries to take the conversation further, immediately go get a round of beer (even if you are having this discussion around the office water cooler). Or, if you have to, fake another heart attack.

Finally, anyone who wants to get their knickers in a knot about our treatment of the overweight in general (i.e., professional curlers), and Hec Gervais in particular, is directed to take a look at the authors' portraits at the back of this book. Yes, Ian and Will are also "physically challenged." Especially around the waist.*

---

* Ian still has a treasured autograph from the great curler himself. Hec signed his name on a pack of Export A cigarettes.

CANADIAN CUISINE

(and how to avoid it)

. . . .

How to Eat
Like a Canadian

*C*ANADIANS HAVE made great contributions to world cuisine. The two
most celebrated being (this is true) baby pablum and frozen peas. The chefs of France are sick with envy over this.
Granted, some critics have had the audacity to suggest
Canadian food is bland, over-processed and sort of mushy.
But we at the HTBAC Institute say pshaw! Pshaw, we say.

Sure, if you let a Canadian get anywhere near a piece
of food they are sure to fling it into a deep fryer. Or cover
it with sugar. Or fling it into a deep fryer and *then* cover
it with sugar. (Admit it; you could go for something deep-
fried and sugar-coated right about now, couldn't you?)

This is why Tim Hortons (a.k.a. Robins, a.k.a. Coffee
Time) represents the peak and the epitome, the acme and
the apex of Canadian cuisine. Everything in a Tim Hortons—including the countertops (completely), the staff
(inevitably) and the customers (eventually)—is covered
with a layer of warm grease and dusted with icing sugar.
The chain itself was named in memory of a hockey player

who died because he was driving dangerously in a sports car. In Canada, this makes him a hero.

> *Question:* Why?
> *Answer:* Who knows?

Sadly, Tim Hortons has, of late, priced itself out of the market. That is, their prices are too damn *low*. Who wants to buy a coffee for less than $3.50? A coffee and a doughnut for a toonie—with change back? Who needs that? Into this gap have stepped several proud chains not afraid of charging more—much more—for their coffee. The leader in Charging More for Coffee has been the U.S.-based Starbucks chain, also known as Second Cup, also known as A.L. Van Houtte.* It remains to be seen whether Tim Hortons will be able to withstand this assault.

Still, there is more to Canadian cuisine than Tim Hortons. Not much more, mind you, but it's still worth exploring, if only to better understand the lesser-known, non-doughnut aspect of the Canadian diet.

BEHOLD THE BREATHTAKING GLORY
THAT IS CANADIAN CUISINE!

One has only to go to that Glorious Forum of Canadian Cuisine to see the splendour, the variety and—yes—the magnificent bounty of the Canadian approach to food. We are speaking, of course, of. . . the FOOD COURT. (*Cue:* Hallelujah chorus and parting clouds.) Hermetically sealed and climate-controlled, where the many varied cultures

---

* Who was, sadly, the passenger in the car that Tim Horton drove off the road.

of the world are reduced to fast food: Is there anything more Canadian than a shopping mall Food Court? What a splendid cornucopia awaits the Food Court denizen! What a dizzying array of choices. Greek! Chinese! Italian! Vietnamese! American! Mexican! Japanese! The glory of the Canadian Food Court is unparalleled.

The greatest cultures on earth have flourished at the crossroads, and the bazaar of modern Canadian life is exemplified by the bustling excitement of the Food Court. The culinary offerings of the world, lukewarm and crusted, sit tantalizingly in their heat trays. All you have to do is grab your own tray and line up!

Now, you may be asking yourself, what about French cuisine? Well, what about it? You want French cuisine, go to France. In Quebec, they don't eat snails and frou-frou entrees. In Quebec, they guzzle spruce beer and wolf down steamed hot dogs. Indeed, *steamés,* as these hot dogs are known, are the National Food of Quebec. If the Quebec School of Culinary Arts ever chose an emblem, it would be a hand holding a steamed hot dog proudly in the air, like a beacon, like a sword. The people in Quebec eat at fast-food emporiums such as Burger King and La Belle Province more often than they ever dine on paté and aubergines. When the Québécois go to France, they ask for ketchup. When they are served Belgian waffles, they ask for syrup. When they go to the beach, they eat corn dogs. It's not for nothing they used to be known as "pepsis."

In Quebec, something that is perfect is described as *c'est chocolat,* and they have a point. After all, other than Molson Ex, what could possibly be better than chocolate? The Québécois slang for "first class" is—this is true, too—

ketchup, proving once again that they are as much North American as they are French.

Yes, the Québécois are hosers just like the rest of us, and any claims to the contrary can be dismissed with a single word: *Florida.* If you want to find out how elevated and sophisticated French Canadians are compared to their uncouth English-Canadian cousins, take a trip to sunny Florida. The inhabitants there know firsthand how urbane and suave, how refined and worldly Canada's French-speaking population is. Speedos? *Oui!* Svelte bodies? *Non.*

Toques, beer, hockey and maple syrup: French or English, we're all still Canadians at heart.

We now present, for your delectation, a handy guide to Canadian cuisine.

Poutine: Quebec's contribution to fine cuisine. French fries covered with cheese curds and gravy. Only 12,486 calories a serving. (Also true: In Quebec, something that's a lot of nonsense is described as *"C'est de la poutine!"*)

Prairie oysters: Western Canada's contribution to fine cuisine. Fried testicle of young bull, consumed mainly in anecdote. (Reportedly tastes like chicken.)

Pemmican: Native Canadian contribution to fine cuisine. Leathery food prepared by Native guides for Hudson's Bay Company traders. Made from pounded buffalo meat, raw fat and cranberries. Tough to chew and hard to swallow, it has a half-life longer than plutonium. Rumoured to be a practical joke played on the whites.

Dulse: Maritimers' contribution to fine cuisine. Tastes like iodine and smells like fish secretions, with the texture and allure of boiled licorice. Rumoured to be a practical joke played on Upper Canadians. "Why, I bet they're so gullible they'd eat these smelly wet weeds I found along the docks." These are the same folks, remember, who routinely try to get people to eat fronds (otherwise known as *fiddleheads*).

Maple syrup: Ketchup may be Canada's Official Condiment, but the sentimental favourite is still *sucre de pays.* Give a Canadian a jug o' maple syrup and they are in hoser heaven, splashing it over anything within striking distance: pancakes, waffles, ice cream, small pets, patio furniture, in-laws, etc. Maple syrup is the great Canadian foodstuff. (The term "foodstuff" being particularly apt when describing Canadian cuisine. "What'cha eatin'?" "Food stuff.")

Canada produces more than 80% of the world's supply of maple syrup, and most of it comes from Quebec, where the people are basically sugar junkies. They're addicted to incredibly sweet foods. Examples include *tarte au sucre* (sugar pie), *trempette* (a piece of bread soaked in maple sugar) and *tire sur la neige* (maple taffy on snow). And let's not forget the very popular and oh-so-disgusting *sucre à la crème,* which is essentially sweetened condensed milk. With sugar added. *"Menum, menum!"* This is what Leonard Cohen was referring to when he talked about "beautiful French girls with terrible teeth."*

There are even—this is true—maple syrup "connoisseurs," who act like wine tasters, only stickier and (we

---

* Another little-known fact. Montreal is also the last major North American city that doesn't fluoridate its water. Again with the teeth. First they addict you to sugar, then they don't provide fluoride. It's like some kind of dental conspiracy.

imagine) chubbier. These connoisseurs sniff, taste and grade maple syrup, ranking it as "sweet," "spicy," "nutty," "flowery," and so on.

"Ah yes, a medium amber—from the Lower St. Lawrence, I believe, Canada No. 2, B Grade if I'm not mistaken. A fine bouquet and impeccable vintage, insouciant yet subtle, cloyingly sweet yet horribly syrupy."

Other contributions that Canada has made to world cuisine include Coffee Crisp ("It's chocolate—and caffeine!"), Catelli ("It's spaghetti sauce—in a can!"), Habitant Pea Soup ("It's pea soup—in a can!") and, of course, Red Rose tea ("It's tea—but only in Canada!").

And you've got to love a country that gave us Coffee Crisp. "Do you know what this chocolate bar needs? A good shot of caffeine." That pretty much sums up the Canadian approach to cuisine. Pass the cheese curds—and mind the dulse!

Lunch with Jan Wong

No discussion of food would be complete without a section on what is, perhaps, the most common dining experience in Canada. Namely: having lunch with Jan Wong.

Here's what Jan Wong does for a living. She invites unsuspecting "celebrities" (in Canada, the term "celebrity" must always include quotation marks) out to "lunch" (ditto) and then she ambushes them. She dices, slices, skewers and skins them. Slowly. She is the Hannibal Lecter of Canadian journalism.

Why should you care? Because eventually every single person in Canada will be required to have lunch with Jan Wong. It's sort of like jury duty. So, to prepare you for your inevitable lunch with the Jan, we at the HTBAC Institute have compiled the definitive guide to defeating the Dragon Lady. The trick is misdirection and cunning. You must use your opponent's strengths against her, as one would with kung fu. The road is hard, Grasshopper. But you can do it. Now—quick! snatch this pebble from my...Okay, best two out of three.

Here, then, are the Five Ways to Defeat Jan Wong.

NUMBER ONE: THE WAY OF THE CRANE
Point to your throat and feign laryngitis, answering every question with only a nod or a shake of the head. An alternate evasive action: If she asks you a particularly probing question, begin to wheeze and choke, then stumble to your feet and attempt to perform the Heimlich manoeuvre on yourself, spewing food across the table before collapsing dramatically onto the floor. (Practice your spewing the night before.)

NUMBER TWO: THE WAY OF THE FOX
Throw her off the scent by "revealing" some fictitious family scandal. Kind of like the Ondaatje brothers, but instead of picking on a real person, invent one. Make up a relative and drop hints that some dark secret is being withheld. For example, when she asks about your family, reply, "They're great ... except for Uncle Louie," then mutter under your breath, "God, how I hate him. Ever since he seduced my fiancée and humiliated me in front of my co-ed macramé class, I have vowed vengeance." Trust us: Jan will be all over that angle like ugly on a moose.

NUMBER THREE: THE WAY OF THE BOAR
In Ian's own words: "Go for it! Eat the mashed potatoes with your fingers, scratch your ass with your fork, wipe your mouth with the

tablecloth. Belch out the national anthem—and then challenge her to top it. Get pissy-eyed drunk and take a swing at the waiter. Grope Jan under the table. Try to force a kiss on her as you leave. Fill out a customer satisfaction card complaining about the service. Go wild!"

NUMBER FOUR: THE WAY OF THE MONKEY
(OR, "IF YOU CAN'T DAZZLE 'EM WITH BRILLIANCE...")

Yodel with your milk. Give every answer in the form of a question. Force her to interview you via a sock puppet named Doodle. Pull a Travis Bickle; after every question narrow your gaze and say, "Are you talking to me? There's no one else at this table, so you must be talking to me." Pretend you're hard of hearing. Make her SCREAM her questions at you. Insist on giving her only your name, rank and serial number. (Make up your rank and change your serial number, just to be safe. And it's better not to give her your real name, either.) Take the Fifth and refuse to answer even the most trivial question on the grounds that it may incriminate you. "Do I want dessert? I refuse to answer that question..." Every five minutes shriek wildly and point over her shoulder. "It's Sondra Gotlieb! Hit the dirt!" Announce that you have allergies to everything, including ice water—and then eat off her plate. With both hands. Go to the bathroom and never return. In an act of incredible arrogance, insist that you be addressed as "Lord Archer." (Oops, that's already been done.) Sing your answers in falsetto. Bog the entire interview down with pregnant pauses. Cross your arms, shake your head and say, "Oooh, that's a tough one" after every question. Two words: whoopee cushion. Break down in tears every time she asks a hard question. Pretend to be someone else. Jan Wong (this is true) once booked an interview with historian Michael Ignatieff only because she got his name confused with novelist Michael Ondaatje. So try to make her think she's screwed up again by adopting an alter ego. "Will Ferguson? No, no, no. The name is Wilf Erguson. I'm a Hollywood stunt double by day—and a masked avenger by night!" Show up dressed in a Masked Avenger costume. Point a finger at her and declare: "In the name of Atwood and Ondaatje, I condemn you! Vengeance is at hand!"

NUMBER FIVE: THE WAY OF THE RAT

Simply put: Incriminating photographs. Never underestimate the power of incriminating photographs. Not that we are suggesting you blackmail Jan into writing nice things about you, but it should be noted that when Will's turn in the barrel came up, the article that followed was not nasty in the least. It was even kind of nice.

And Jan, if you're reading this: the negatives are in the mail.

CHAPTER 7 SUMMARY: WHAT YOU'VE LEARNED SO FAR

Canadian food will rot your teeth and make you fat. At which point, you will have no choice but to take up curling. It's the circle of life.

8

MATING
RITUALS

. . . .

How to Be as Romantic

as a Canadian

EDITOR'S NOTE: This chapter will contain an examination and in-depth discussion of the state of romance in Canada. It will NOT be usurped by Will as an excuse to plead with his fellow Canadians for an increase in kinky sex. The publisher has made this amply clear on several—

ATTENTION: WE INTERRUPT THIS CHAPTER
TO BRING YOU AN IMPORTANT PUBLIC MESSAGE.

SEX, CANOES AND EVIL EMPIRES:
A PLEA FROM WILL TO HIS FELLOW CANADIANS

Comrades! What this country needs is a good perversion. Something kinky and twisted that we can call our very own. In England it's nannies and riding crops, in America it's inflatable breasts, in France it's body odour and warm snails—and trust me, you don't even want to *know* about the Japanese. But what has Canada given the world? What have we contributed to the general decadence of society at large? Not much, I can tell you. We don't even have a National Fetish (unless you count Royal Commissions; see Chapter 15).

Pierre Berton once declared that a Canadian is someone "who knows how to make love in a canoe." But Pierre was just bragging. Or lying. If average Canadians ever tried to "pull a Berton" they'd end up looking like Mr. Canoe Head. (For those of you unfamiliar with His Canoe-Headedness, Mr. Canoe Head was a superhero whose head was permanently stuck inside a canoe. But it was okay, because he wore disguises to hide it. You know, fake beards and whatnot.) In his 1978 collection, *Lependu,* poet Don McKay writes, "There are but forty-seven known sexual acts which can be accomplished in the thwarted canoe (*Kamacanada Sutra,* Ryerson Press, 1917), many of them solitary."

I'm sure your reaction to reading this was much the same as mine: "Where can I get a copy of the *Kamacanada Sutra* and does it include pictures?" Sadly, in my extensive search of secondhand bookstores and public libraries, I was unable to turn up a single copy, and I fear that the book may not really exist.

But I did come across a faded copy of an actual book called—and I quote—*The First Original Unexpurgated Canadian Book of Sex and Adventure,* published back in those madcap, swinging seventies. And all it cost me was two bucks and a funny look from the clerk.

Choked with excitement, I hurried home, closed the blinds and curled up beneath the covers to read about Canadian "sex and adventure." Let me stress, once again, that this is a real book, published in hardcover, no less.

Alas, I knew I was in for a letdown when I flipped it open and saw the following heading: THE TEN SEXIEST BANK PRESIDENTS IN CANADA. *Bank presidents!* With a sense of panic creeping in, I began turning the pages frantically, searching for something—anything—that was even mildly arousing. EIGHT REASONS WHY CANADIAN MEN MAKE GOOD HUSBANDS . . . no, no, no! TEN IMPORTANT POINTS OF ETIQUETTE TO REMEMBER ABOUT CANADIAN WEDDINGS. *Aaaarghh!* THE TEN MOST SEXLESS MAGAZINES IN CANADA. That's right, sex*less!* I'd been duped!

The book slid from my hand and fell to the floor. Disheartened and depressed, I went down to the lake to spend a few moments alone, just me and my canoe. In fairness, I did learn some interesting things from that book. For example, did you know that the most common time for sex in Canada is—when else?—on Saturday evenings, after *Hockey Night in Canada.* (Or it was in the 1970s, at least.) Or did you know that the *least* sexy politician in Canada is Joe Clark? (Okay, so that one you already knew.) How about the fact that Reggie Leach was once the Ninth-Sexiest Hockey Player in the NHL? Betcha didn't know *that.* (Do you see the kind of invaluable information you are gaining from reading *How to Be a Canadian* rather than spending your time doing something more productive, like, say, staring at the ceiling?)

But gems such as these aside, the *Canadian Book of Sex and Adventure* ("Original and Unexpurgated!") still failed to answer that single, nagging question: "What has Canada given to the perverts of the world?" The Scottish kilt introduced cold-climate transvestitism (i.e., the "shrivel syndrome"), the French have a kiss named in their honour, and the Spanish have a fly. But not Canada. This lack must have something to do with our colonial past transposed against modern anxieties, or maybe the fact that we have eight months of winter.

How, then, is one to sum up the sexual predilections of an entire nation? Well, at this point, in my continuing quest to use the pithy quotes of others to save me the effort of coming up with witty insights of my own, I am reminded of the words of Claude T. Bissell, who said—and I quote— "Canadians move slowly, but when they are aroused they move with remarkable speed. Our way of life is puritanism touched by orgy."

Hot damn, a puritan orgy! Just the kind of erotic oxymoron you'd expect from the nation that gave us Progressive Conservatives. But Mr. Bissell's analysis applies only to *English* Canada—although I personally, as an English Canadian, have never once been invited to an orgy, puritan or otherwise. I did spend one New Year's Eve outside of Toronto's City Hall pressed up against approximately 50,000 fellow Canadians of all genders and inclinations, but I'm not sure if that counts.

French Canadians, contrary as always, are completely the opposite. *Their* way of life is one of orgy touched by puritanism (hence their Machiavellian sign laws and live sex shows). And unlike their cousins in France, French Canadians do take showers. Often right up there on stage.

So, to sum up:

English Canadians: puritanism touched by orgy
French Canadians: orgy tainted by puritanism

(French Canadians mock us, you know. They call us blockheads—*têtes carrées*—and are convinced, absolutely convinced, that we are hopelessly unhip. This simply is not true. After all, didn't English Canada give the world Anne Murray and Paul Anka? They tell jokes about us as well. Mean, nasty ones like "How many English Canadians does it take to have an orgy?" Answer: "One or two.")

Anyway, there I was, despairing over ever being able to finish this chapter, agonizing over ever being able to find something distinctly Canadian involving sex or passion, languishing over a beer, when suddenly I saw it! Across the bar! A paperback book held aloft by a solitary lady at the next table. (This is almost a true story.) This lady, obviously in dire need of some passion, was reading. . . a Harlequin romance.

There it was in front of me: the place where the repressed sexuality of Canadian women goes. In men this repression manifests itself directly as Really Big Towers (*see* CN Tower, misplaced pride in), but in women, it is rerouted into romance novels.

Reading Harlequin romances is the Big Female Mystery, as not a single woman will admit to buying them, yet billions and billions are sold every year. Only a nation like Canada, a nation seething with bottled rage and lust, only a nation of such secret dark desires, only a nation of squareheads such as we could possibly have produced Harlequin romances, and—get ready to put on your party hats and boogie—WE DID.

The Harlequin saga began in 1949, when a man named Richard Bonnycastle founded a small pulp-paperback publishing company in Winnipeg. Harlequin Books, as it was known, originally published anything they could get their hands on. ("A wide variety of genres" is, I believe, how the press release put it.) Their early titles included such well-loved· classics as *This Gun for Gloria* and *Wreath for a Redhead*. But the company later decided to focus solely on romance, because, as Mr. Bonnycastle's wife, Mary, pointed out, readers really seemed to enjoy those "nice little books with happy endings."

The next thing you know, Harlequin—and I'm trying to find a way to put this nicely—began to spread like a giant, malignant octopus, swallowing other companies whole and spreading its tentacles and trademark (a cute little juggler known affectionately as "Joey") like a dark plague into other languages and other nations, poisoning wells and conquering world markets until today it reigns undisputed as the world's largest romance publisher, standing astride the globe in eighteen languages and more than a hundred countries, head back and laughing. *Bwahahahaha!*

If that didn't unnerve you, maybe this will: *Half* of Harlequin readers are college-educated women. And over 200 million women worldwide are faithful readers. These women are all around us, yet there is no way to tell who they are. Governor General Adrienne Clarkson could very well be a secret Harlequin reader. Deborah Grey, certainly. Sheila Copps, probably. Perhaps even *Post* columnist Christie Blatchford. They might all be secret Harlequin readers! Egads. It's like some spooky body-changer movie. Men, listen to me! Your very own mother/sister/wife/girlfriend could have a whole closet full of Harlequins *and you would never know!* Unless, of course, you clean the closet. Which will never happen.

Which brings me back to my original point, which was—let me see—sex in canoes. You are probably wondering what this stuff about Harlequin has to do with anything. It's simple: Although Canada may not have contributed much to world sexuality per se, when it comes to Romance, we've cornered the market! *Bwahahahaha!*

WE NOW RETURN TO OUR REGULAR PROGRAMMING.

CHAPTER 8 SUMMARY: WHAT YOU'VE LEARNED SO FAR

At this point, there is only one thing we would like to add: The worst Canadian movie ever made, and perhaps the worst movie of all time, was *Leopard in the Snow,* based on a Harlequin romance and starring Keir Dullea (of *2001: A Space Odyssey* fame) and Margot Kidder. This feature film was actually released in theatres, but is now tragically unavailable on video or DVD, so you'll have to take our word on how awfully, horrifically bad this flick was. Or. If you are an aficionado of bad Canadian cinema (which is pretty much any film made here between, oh, 1971 and 1989), you might want to sign our online e-mail petition at *fergusonbrothers@canada.com.* Send us a message to say, "Yes! I want to have access to the WORST CANADIAN MOVIE EVER MADE." We will then gather up these heartfelt pleas and send them off to the people at Harlequin in an attempt to get them to re-release this timeless classic on the big screen. Honestly, it's that bad. It's so bad you have to see it. It's so bad it's got "cult classic" written all over it. It could be our very own Canadian version of *Plan 9 from Outer Space.* Those Harlequin folks don't realize it, but they're sitting on a gold mine.

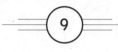

9

SEX

(Note: This chapter has been

sealed for your protection)

. . . .

*O*NLY PEOPLE in Newfoundland have sex. Everyone else just talks about it. Incessantly. So don't be shy. Pipe up and speak your mind. There is nothing you can't discuss in Canada when it comes to sex. You can call up strangers and say, "Hi! We're taking a survey and we want to talk to you about sex! Do you like sex? How much do you like sex? How often do you have sex?"

Do not talk about love, however. That makes Canadians uncomfortable.

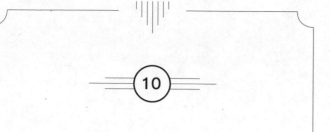

BEER

. . . .

How to Drink Like

a Canadian

WHY BEER?

Beer was not invented in Canada. It was not perfected in Canada. Canadian beer is *not* world famous, and Canadians, unlike the Germans, have *not* distinguished themselves by the great quantities they quaff. In fact, when it comes to per capita beer consumption, Canada is not even in the Top 10 among Western nations. As beer drinkers, Canadians are wimps. And yet, in spite of this, beer is a point of eternal pride among Canadians and is, in fact, an essential item in the Standard Canadian Identi-Kit.

A sociologist—particularly an incompetent one—might explain the Canadian affinity for beer something like this: For all its tourist-brochure–encoded imagery of majestic mountains and rugged malamutes, Canada is a hopelessly middle-class, suburban nation whose average citizens couldn't pick a moose out of a police lineup. If Canadian society were an actor, it would be described as having "bland good looks." The Kevin Costner of nations, that's us.

Understandably, most Canadians would rather cling to an outdated stereotype: that of the rough-and-ready, frontier-bred Canadian, big of heart and blue of collar—an outdoorsy, affable, individualistic yet law-abiding, broad-chested guy. Beer, then, is a psychological prop in this national lumberjack role-playing game. A totemistic touchstone, if you will. So you can see just how incompetent a sociologist would have to be to come up with such a theory. (We're sure glad *we* didn't suggest it.)

No. The Canadian fetish for beer goes deeper than mere role-playing. Much deeper. It springs from the dark, musty, mildewed corners of the national psyche. It strikes at the very heart of the Great Canadian Inferiority Complex vis-à-vis (who else?) the Americans. Simply put, brewing beer is one of the few things that Canadians do better than Americans. Which may also explain the irresistible attraction between beer and curling.

Sure, the average Englishman may sniff with disdain at the mild brown lager that is our National Drink, but what do Canadians care? It is not the Brits that we want to beat. Hell, they drink their beer *warm,* for Chrissake! A Canadian wouldn't drink a warm beer if they had just been pulled out of a snowbank in Saskatoon. I'm sorry, but "Give me a warm one!" just doesn't scan.

POP QUIZ

Canadian beer is stronger than American beer. True or false?

True—but just barely. The numbers on the beer labels lie. The average Canadian beer is a mere 0.5% stronger than the average American beer. You see, Americans use a different method of measuring alcohol percentage than do Canadians, so a 5% Canadian beer is actually *equal* to a 4% American. Not a big difference. Negligible, in fact. We know, we know. It goes against everything Canadians have been taught to believe. Canadian beer really *isn't* that much stronger than American. (Check out *Jackson's Pocket Guide to Beer* if you don't believe us.)

Nope. Canadian beer is not strong. The Swiss mock it. The Germans use it to gargle. And the Irish? Ah yes, the Irish. Try quaffing a "meal in itself" Guinness if you want strong. You can float small change on the surface of real Guinness stout. Patrons regularly get Guinness stuck between their teeth. Seabirds often tragically get caught in Guinness slicks and have to be rescued by conservationists.

It isn't the amount of alcohol per bottle that gives Canadian beer its charm. It is, quite simply: *the taste.* Canadian beer tastes better than American beer. Period. This is the one indisputable, self-evident fact of which Canadians are certain. Had Descartes been Canadian instead of whatever he was (French or Belgian or something), he would have started with beer when he formulated his first principle of philosophical certainty, and the fact that Canadian beer is superior to American would now be the foundation of modern Western thought.

Instead of "I think, therefore I am," Descartes's maxim would have been something like "I think I need another beer, therefore I am—going to have one, that is."

So why does Canadian beer taste better? The answer, as always, lies rooted deep in our collective past. The history of Canadian beer reveals early cultural influences, and indeed, one could argue that to know beer is to know

Canada, although one would probably have to be drunk at the time.

Beer first took hold in Canada in the eighteenth century, when it was introduced by Irish, English and Scottish settlers who set up small breweries that produced *ale*. Ale is made by fermenting the yeast at the top of the brew, a method that produces the heavy and bitter drink still preferred in Britain today.

In America, however, it was the Slavic and German immigrants who first mass-produced beer, and they preferred *lager*—a pale, light drink made with bottom-fermenting yeast.* (*Stout,* meanwhile, is whatever guck they can scrape off the bottom of the barrel after everything else has been taken. This is all true. We take our beer seriously here at the HTBAC Institute.)

These two cultural backgrounds, one British and the other German, are reflected today in the names of the leading North American breweries: Molson and Carling O'Keefe on one side of the border; Schlitz, Pabst and Anheuser-Busch on the other. Labatt, the other major brewery in Canada, was also founded by an Englishman, despite the French-sounding name.

In time, tastes changed. Canadians may have begun with ale, and the Americans with lager, but over the years the American lager grew more and more anemic until it finally became the pale *eau d'bier* they now call "lite," which greatly confuses Canadian visitors, who see it as a redundancy. ("*Lite* American beer? Is there any other kind?")

---

* It is pronounced "lagger," NOT "logger." We don't care what the dictionary says.

Meanwhile, in the Great White North, Canadian tastes changed as well. Breweries here gradually abandoned ale and began producing lager instead. But the early preference for ale lingers on in the darker, tangier quality of Canadian beer. Hence the present difference in taste between American and Canadian beer (i.e., Canadian beer *has* taste). With current trends, Canadians have been drifting towards draft beer and the Americans towards beige water.

American beer, as they say, is like making love in a canoe. If you don't know the punchline to this joke, find someone who does. If you already know it, chances are you yourself are Canadian. So, grab a cold one and pull up a seat.

SCREECH (AND OTHER POISON)

We would be remiss in discussing the refined tastes of Canadians with regard to alcoholic beverages (meaning: beer) without mentioning a few regional variations.

Quebeckers, for one, make *le caveau du dépanneur* their wine cellar of choice. When Will was living in Quebec back in the 1980s, the favoured drink was Cuvée des Patriotes, which was sometimes jokingly referred to as "wine." Beloved as much for its low price as for its affordability, Cuvée des Patriotes was best drunk straight from the bottle, with a crumpled paper bag covering the label. (Even winos were embarrassed to be seen lowering their standards to drink Cuvée des Patriotes.) When Pope John Paul II came to Quebec, it was said that one of the miracles he performed was turning Cuvée des Patriotes into wine. Sadly, the glory days of Cuvée are long gone. Another cultural icon fades from view.

In the West, the famed drink is the Calgary Red Eye: beer and an egg—or tomato juice or something. No one actually drinks it. It's more urban legend than real. Calgary was also the city where the Caesar was invented. It's true. It happened at a local hotel, when an enterprising bartender said, "You know what we need in a drink? You know what would make for a really refreshing beverage? Clamato, Tabasco sauce and salt."

But the real triumph of regional beverages is Newfoundland's drink of choice: *screech*. Screech is the bane of every weak-kneed, tender-footed tourist ever to stumble—by mistake—into Newfoundland. Screech! The elemental fire, the sound of fingernails on blackboard, the cry of the Valkyries, the cackle of witch-fire, the—well, you get the idea.

Screech, for those of you fortunate enough to have avoided it until now, is the national drink of Newfoundland. Rum. Cheap rum. Cheap *Jamaican* rum. Wrathful, firebreathing, eyeball-bleeding, down the hatch, sear-yer-gut and melt-yer-eyebrows Jamaican rotgut. One of the great pastimes of Newfoundlanders (who are, let's face it, a particularly sadistic people) is to torment visitors with screech.

Centuries ago, Newfoundlanders began trading salt fish to Jamaica in return for rum, and the arrangement was so mutually beneficial that the bilateral "rum for salt fish" trade has more or less continued to this day. Jamaican rum is now the mainstay of Newfoundlanders everywhere, and salt fish is now the national dish of Jamaica. The Jamaicans got the better part of the deal. The original rum—and to be frank, we have trouble imagining this—was actually much stronger and far more lethal than the stuff labelled as such and sold in government liquor stores today. Today's screech is snorted at by real Newfoundlanders, who consider it "just so much coloured water."

Question: Are they insane?
Answer: Yes.

They even have a harsher drink called calabogus (a.k.a. "callibogus," a.k.a. "Quick, call an ambulance!"), which is a mix of screech, spruce beer and molasses.

What, no Tabasco sauce?

CHAPTER 10 SUMMARY: WHAT YOU'VE LEARNED SO FAR

Canadians like beer. In Quebec they like cheap wine, and in Newfoundland they like cheap rum. And that's about it. That is the educational essence of this chapter. So we would like to take this opportunity instead to introduce you to a fun-filled party game. It's called "Drinkin' and NOT Drivin'," and it goes like this: Have a beer or maybe twelve (it's more fun if you're really, really. . . uh, tipsy) and then stagger into a restaurant or twenty-four-hour convenience store with a set of keys in your hand and berate the clerk on duty as you loudly demand directions back to your car. When the cops show up, tell 'em it was just a fun drinking game, that you (heaven forbid) had no intention of driving while under the influence, and that the keys in your hand are actually to your locker at the gym. Then, once the officers have gotten over their amusement at your jaunty prank, go outside, unlock your car and try to drive away. . . The next morning, after you are released, take a taxicab home.

ART AND STUFF

. . . .

How to Be as Cultured

as a Canadian

*N*o, no, no. Canadian culture isn't boring. *You're* boring. It's your fault Canadian artists have to wait tables, and it's your fault the CBC is struggling ("Today on *Hot Type:* Authors Earnestly Discuss Their Books in an Earnest Manner with an Oh So Earnest Host. The Excitement Never Ends, Here on the CBC!"). This is the first rule in Canada regarding the arts. If people don't tune in or buy your book or come to your play, blame the public.

Here's just a sampler of Canada's outstanding artistic achievements in the fields of music, dance and theatre:

The Edmonton Symphony Orchestra

Biggest claim to fame? They once recorded a live album with the profoundly pretentious rock band Procul Harum. There is a section of "A Whiter Shade of Pale" where the bassoons come in for a solo that will take your breath away.

The National Ballet of Canada

The greatest moment in the history of this illustrious dance company came when they assisted Russian superstar dancer Mikhail Barishnikov in defecting from the USSR. By way of expressing his gratitude, Barishnikov performed a couple of solos with the company before heading off to fame and fortune in the U.S.A. If you caught his performance in the movie *White Nights,* well, it probably took your breath away.

The Manitoba Theatre Centre

One of the highlights for this theatre company had to be when ex-pat Canadian thespian Keanu Reeves put his burgeoning movie career on hold to appear in the title role of *Hamlet.* The entire run of the show was sold out in less than forty-eight hours, and fans of the alleged actor came from as far away as Japan and Europe to watch him perform the part of the melancholy Dane. Reeves delivered a mildly competent performance, but his screen persona had so lowered the bar, as far as artistic expectations go, that most people who caught the show felt that although he didn't actually take your breath away, he didn't suck either.

What do these renowned Canadian institutions of High Art have in common? Well, first of all, they each have a long and storied history of providing high-quality artistry that has earned them stellar international reputations. Second, they are all broke. Or, rather, "very nearly perpetually on the edge of financial oblivion." Which is to say, they rely very heavily on the whimsical nature of various levels of government funding in order to keep their doors open.

Which explains why, as our examples above indicate, they have resorted to various weird stunts and wacky shenanigans to raise their profile with the general public. (What could be weirder or wackier than helping the best ballet dancer in the world escape to freedom and not signing him to a long-term contract? What *were* they thinking?) And, of course, they are also an intricate part of the warp and weave of the rich fabric that makes up the tablecloth and matching doilies of Canada's diverse cultural tapestry.

There's art everywhere in Canada. The entire country is dripping with it. For instance, it turns out that there are art galleries located in every major city in Canada. And in Regina, too. Wander into one of these places and you will be exposed to every type of art imaginable, with the exception of work by Ken Danby, who is either a little too realistic artistically, or a little too successful financially, to warrant exhibition in public galleries.

Or let's say you want to attend a dance performance instead. Maybe you're defecting from a Communist country and you want to suss out your options. There is classical (i.e., ballet, e.g., the Royal Winnipeg, Les Ballets Jazz de Montréal). Or, if you're looking for something a little less formal, you might be interested in checking out a contemporary or modern dance company (e.g., Danny Grossman, Pounds/per/square/inch).

How to choose? Easy. It all boils down to this. Would you prefer to watch women in froofy tutus and men in anatomically revealing tights prancing about the stage, or would you rather watch naked girls writhing about in nothing but body paint? So it's settled, then. Naked dancers and body paint it is.

You may also want to buy a ticket to one of Canada's fine ethnic dance troupes, like Edmonton's Shumka Dancers (who specialize in Ukrainian dance) or Kajifka (African tribal movement and dance) or the Swirlin' Dervish Amish Dancers (they don't actually play music or dance or anything; they just stand around in a circle and shun you with a baleful gaze). But if you really want to see fancy footwork, your best bet is still to make your way to the Parliament Buildings in Ottawa and watch the politicians dance around the issues. For maximum entertainment, try to arrive during Question Period.

We would now like to look more closely at four specific areas of Canadian cultural expression: music, theatre, film and literature. These worthwhile endeavours reflect positive social values that—*hey!!* Where are you going? Get back here!

MUSIC

There are two general types of music to choose from in Canada. There is the type of music that no one listens to but everyone admires. Or the type that everyone listens to but no one will admit they admire. That is, there is classical music and then there is non-classical (or "popular") music.

Classical Music

Forget the actual music. The music isn't important. No one really cares about the music. We have that on the inside authority of an anonymous source deep within the world of Canadian music.* What *is* important is the small circle of music reviewers. Yessir. When it comes to classical music,

---

* Again, that would be Ferguson brother #3, Sean.

the role of the critic cannot be overemphasized. Well, yes, actually. It *could* be overemphasized. We *could* say that music critics are more important than oxygen, or that they have saved small children from burning buildings, or that they have selflessly discovered a cure for cancer—or even that they have contributed something useful to society. But music reviewers—like theatre critics and book reviewers—do serve an important function, in the same way that sucker fish probably serve some sort of function when they feed off the effluence of larger fish. Not that Ian (theatre), Will (books) or Sean (music) are bitter. No sir.

Anyway. In the world of Canadian classical music, here's how it works: The audience dresses up and goes to the concert, and then—this is where the excitement really builds—they hurry home and . . . they wait. They wait until the review appears. They then read the review to discover whether or not they liked the music. Concerts in Canada are about social profile; the music is just an annoyance. Hence the important role of the music critic to do the listening and evaluation on behalf of the audience, who, let's face it, have more important things to do.

Popular Music

If we're going to talk about popular music, let's talk about music that really is popular. Let's talk country. Let's talk western. With Shania Twain shaking the charts, we at the IITBAC Institute thought we would jump on the bandwagon as well.* (And with a name like "Shania Twain," she didn't have much of a choice, did she? What else could she be, except a country and western singer? "Hello, I'll be your

* "Yee" and "haw."

neurosurgeon today. The name's Twain, Shania Twain." Can't see it.)

Country music is about cheatin' and drinkin' and runnin' around, and not enjoying any of it. The songs have titles like "Rocking Chairs and Tomatoes—That Bernice Canned for Me" and "Why Don't You Love Me Like I Loved You Before?".

Sample song: "Cheap Bacon on a Grill," by I. Ferguson

> I was sittin', eatin' breakfast
> And feelin' mighty blue,
> Why'd you steal my pick-up, darlin'
> And my old dog Blue?
> But I started thinkin'
> As I sat there drinkin'
> I could feel my love a'shrinkin'
> Like cheap bacon on a grill.

Other styles of popular music include Cape Breton fiddle tunes. Or rather "tune." There is only one Cape Breton fiddle tune in existence. It goes like this: *diddle-diddle-diddle-diddle-diddle-dee* (repeat).

And then there is the Canadian crooner song, as exemplified by a strange stick-insect woman from Quebec who shall remain nameless (Celine Dion). Once Celine latches onto a note, you can't shake her off. She's like a Rottweiler on a kitten. She will hold that note forever and squeeze it like a lemon, till she wrings out every ounce of overwrought emotion possible. *"I neeeeeeeeed you, I feeeeeeeeeeeel youuuuuuuuuuuuu."* It can take Celine upwards of two days to finish a song. Heck, she's still trying to wrap up her performance at the Millennium Concert. (Remember that? In Celine's mind, the dawn of the Second Millennium was of less significance than the fact that Celine was—ohmygod!—retiring. At least for now.)

Celine Dion is, of course, a mutant. (That was her in the opening scene of the *X-Men* movie.) No real human being can sing like that. For average slobs, the musician of choice is Bryan Adams—who has been around, by our calculations, since forever. If you want to become a star in Canada, you could do worse than follow Bryan's shining example.

Special Bonus! How to Write a Bryan Adams Song

Simple. Only three elements are needed: crashing, over-the-top guitar riffs; a loud, raspy voice; and lyrics stuffed full of clichés. Also note Bryan's clever use of "gonna" and "wanna." Every song Mr. Adams has ever written contains the word "gonna" or "wanna" somewhere in the lyrics. Hence, the Ultimate Bryan Adams Song would be titled . . .

"I'm Gonna Wanna Gonna Go," by Bryan Adams
(as interpreted by W. Ferguson)

Me and the boys, we were really cool
We were the wild ones after school.
They said don't sweat it,
Don't walk on the grass,
Like father, like son,
Time goes so fast.
(*chorus*)
Now, I'm gonna wanna gonna go—tonight!
That's right. I'm gonna wanna gonna go—I'm gonna!

Most depressing thought of this entire chapter? Unlike virtually every other artist in Canada, Bryan Adams has relied solely on his talent. As far as we know, he never received a single Canada Council grant, nor did he benefit from any of the CRTC's parochial Can-content laws. Bryan became a huge international star purely on the strength of his music. He's a "people's star." In other words, it's all your fault.

THEATRE

In Canada, there are six different types of theatre company for you to choose from:

I. Commercial Theatre

Located in Toronto, Vancouver and Montreal only. Not to be confused with some of the larger non-profit theatres, which, despite their not-for-profit designation, are equally interested in making money. Commercial theatres offer epic musicals full of special effects and spectacle. Here's how to tell. If a helicopter lands onstage or a chandelier crashes from the ceiling at a key dramatic moment, chances are you are attending a commercial theatre production. If, however, the helicopter is portrayed by an actor running around frantically beating his fists against his chest or the falling chandelier occurs offstage with the actors pointing to the wing and shouting, "Look! A giant chandelier has fallen to the ground . . . just offstage!", you are probably at a smaller, non-profit theatre.

The tickets to commercial theatre cost a lot of money, more than the cost of an actual helicopter ride, in fact. But the good part is that you get to feel very patriotic by saying things like "Wow, did you know that with the exception of the playwright, the composer, the director, the choreographer, the designer and the two lead actors, the rest of the cast and crew are completely Canadian?"

2. Government-Funded Regional Theatre, Large

Every big city has one, and they can usually be found in a convenient downtown location where parking costs— well, about as much as a helicopter ride. Large government-funded regional theatres function like big industrial bakeries. They're in the bulk business, and they present a consistent, if predictable, recipe of Neil Simon, Noel Coward, the odd musical and assorted plays that were hot on Broadway or in the West End four or five seasons ago. Tickets will cost you almost as much as you'd pay at a commercial theatre, but everybody involved in the show will be Canadian. Except the artistic director. He will be from England.

3. Government-Funded Regional Theatre, Small

Similar to above, only "edgier." And what, per chance, does "edgier" mean? It means they will build their season around a single play—that was hot off-Broadway four or five seasons ago. In Canada, this is considered cutting-edge. These theatres also commission new works by Canadian writers. By law, these plays will be set in the prairies. And they will have titles like *The Wheat Is High* or *42 Short Plays about Gabriel Dumont*. Tickets will be half the price of those at the larger theatres, and the artistic director will be Canadian—and easily recognized. He (or she) will be the person who has to unplug the toilet during intermission.

4. Festivals, Large

These are, effectively, huge repertory theatre companies that specialize in the works of one particular playwright and related writings from around the same era. William Shakespeare or George Bernard Shaw. That kind of thing. Tickets cost an arm and a leg, but they're worth every limb, we say, if only because you'll be able to shout, "Hey! That guy from the Canadian Tire ad is playing Polonius." The artistic directors will be of British origin, but most of them will have taken out Canadian citizenship by now. Get them to autograph your copy of this book. They'll sign anything, including their life, away. You will find them at the bar during interval, in a festive Faustian funk, drinking with a certain raw desperation.

5. Festivals, Small

These are also called "fringe" festivals (as in "lunatic" or "benefits"). Fringe festivals are spreading across the country faster than fungus in a locker room. Low ticket prices, independent productions, and lots of first-time playwrights, actors and directors: basically this type of festival functions like a farm team for the bigger houses. The artistic director of the festival will be a woman, and you will recognize her by the huge bags under her eyes and the constant use of her cell phone to deal with yet another emergency.

A warning. The quality and content of fringe shows can vary widely (and wildly). Necrophilia and the true nature of love, that sort of thing. So don't attend if you're easily shocked and/or bored. Indeed, at many fringe shows you can be both—*at the very same time*. "I was never so shocked in my life! Or so bored!"

6. So-Called Dinner So-Called Theatre

Here, for around the same ticket price that a large govern-ment-funded regional theatre would charge, you not only get a show, you also get "food." (Note the use of quotation marks.) The play itself is probably going to be a tired old British farce with a title like *Ooh, That's Me Bum, Guv'ner!*, and it's going to feature some washed-up American sit-com star in the lead role, but hey. . . have you checked out the buffet? Some dinner theatres also have the actors waiting on tables "in character," which seems sensible, since most of the best waiters tend to be actors. And vice versa.

So get out there and become a regular theatregoer. If you don't believe that the arts should be subsidized, then spend your money at a dinner theatre or go to your local fringe festival. Chances are nobody involved is making any money. Or, if you prefer to support individual artists, at the very least you can give the waiter a decent tip.

FILM

If there's one thing that Canadians know how to do, it's to produce documentaries, especially biographies of artists and writers. The National Film Board has won more than forty Oscars just by working their way through the Group of Seven.

Documentaries are one thing; regular films are another. Canada doesn't really have a star system. In fact, being a celebrity in Canada is a good way to assure one's ano-nymity. (The FBI's Witness Protection Program routinely places people as celebrities within the Canadian film industry.)

Many Canadians aren't even *aware* there is a Canadian film industry. "Canadian *film*?" they will say, speaking in italics for emphasis. "I wasn't even *aware*. I didn't even know it *existed*." There is, and it does. Look at Atom Egoyan. Or that other guy. The one who made that movie about the guy who kills himself because of that thing that happened. And let's not forget *Margaret's Museum*. What a laugh fest that was! In fact, the Canadian film industry holds a ceremony every year to celebrate the very best in Canadian cinema. They then give each other awards. Nobody watches the telecast, and nobody has seen any of the movies, and the ceremony itself is called the GENIES, which is an acronym for "Gosh, Everyone Nominated Is Employed at Starbucks!"

CANADIAN LITERARY ENDEAVOURS
(OR, "COMING SOON TO A REMAINDER BIN NEAR YOU!")

Let's face it, Canadian writers are a breed apart. God-like, good-looking, sophisticated, smooth and reputedly well-endowed: Is there anyone alive who does not envy the status and glory that is the Canadian author? (This is a rhetorical question; do not attempt to answer it.)

You may even want to pursue the writing life yourself and experience the many joys and benefits of a literary lifestyle firsthand. For starters, you get to work in your underwear. And let's not forget the Scratch Yourself Anytime You Want To factor. Try doing that in your standard office and see how far you get.

Now, if you are going to write a CANADIAN NOVEL, you must first decide which type you want to write: the Dysfunctional Family Novel or the Pouty Young Urban Male Novel.

A handy checklist follows. These are the things that book reviewers will be looking for, and it is very important that you *fulfill their expectations*.

Setting

Setting is important. It has to be bleak and foreboding: maybe Cape Breton or outport Newfoundland or a cabin in northern Ontário. (To judge by the output of Canadian novelists, half the young urban male population is hiding out in cabins in northern Ontario.) *Note:* Even if you choose to write a Young Ironic Male Sardonic Angst novel, the setting must still be remote and bleak. In Canada, even urban novels have rural settings.

In fact, the only noticeable difference between the Dysfunctional Family Novel and the Sullen Young Male Disconnectedness Novel is that in the Sullen Young Male Novel, you should try to work a brand name or pop-culture reference into every sentence. For example:

Dysfunctional Family Novel:
Dale put on his jacket and went outside.

Sullen Young Male *Novel:*
Dale closed his iMac, put on his Dicanni Italian-cut overcoat, and then, hitting the mute on his Aiwa digital sound system, he put a Kellogg's Pop Tart[TM] in the Toastamatic 2000 and went outside. In his brand-name shoes.

Plot

Avoid this at all costs. Narrative storylines, where things actually *happen,* are now considered "crass." Instead, the characters should just sort of mope from scene to scene, maybe staring into the distance now and then to remember events that happened long before. You don't want a sense of forward momentum in a novel. You want "atmosphere." Most Canadian novels are built around a series of unmotivated flashbacks. Let's keep it that way, shall we?

Humour

God, no. Instead of humour, you want irony. And lots of it! Your book should be drenched in irony. Soaked in it, even. When someone squeezes your book, irony should ooze out from between the pages. It should reek of postmodern alienation and ennui. The more postmodern the better. (*See* Brand names, the ironic use of. Meaning the author gave a brand name a plug but didn't get any payment for it. The fool.)

Character

In Canadian novels the men—especially the father figures—should be brooding alcoholics, or brooding *violent* alcoholics, or pathetic losers who aren't really alcoholic but are still quite pathetic, or recovering alcoholics, or violent losers, or brooding pathetic recovering alcoholics who are also violent.

The main female character must be victimized. That goes without saying. She *has* to be victimized. But here's the thing—she should also be empowered. That's right. In Canadian novels, you get to have it both ways: "empowered victims."

Handy tip! Write about a family gathering, a funeral or some sort of homecoming. That's the easiest way to bring characters together without having to construct a plot. And make sure to include the free-spirited sister, the recovering alcoholic brother, the other sister (the one who gave up on her dreams and is married to an abusive and/or aloof man) and—last but not least—the standard-issue abusive and/or aloof father figure. Add to the mix some cryptic dialogue about a past betrayal, maybe a dark secret or two, and half-bake at 40°F. Do you see how these things just write themselves?

Style
Keep it simple. Stark. Unfurnished. Underwritten. Subject + verb + object: again and again and again and again. svo. svo. Stick to the bare minimum offered by the English language. Do not use adverbs. And if you have to use adjectives, keep them short and simple and obvious to the point of redundancy (i.e., "blue sky," "white clouds," "wet rain," "unfaithful husband").

Example: "She opened the window. The sky was blue. White clouds were reflected in the cold water. She closed the window. She sat on a green chair. She sighed."

Now then, let's see this in action. (Though, of course, when we say "action" we are speaking figuratively. This is Canadian literature we're talking about, after all.) Here is a scene from a novel in progress, set in a small fishing cove in Newfoundland. Or possibly Cape Breton.

Martha stood up. The storm was coming in. She went outside. She began to take the laundry from the line. Shane was waiting. He was always waiting.

"It will never dry," he said. The sheets were white against the blackening sky. The water was blue and cold.

"They will dry," she said. "They will dry. In time."

"It's cold," he said.

She turned away. "Winter," she said. "It's always cold in winter." She thought of the cellar. The smell of potatoes. The feel of her innocence being destroyed. Forever. The funeral and/or family reunion was next Friday. Would *he* be there too?

She looked back at the house. It was a good house. Not a great house. But still, not bad. As far as houses went.

Chart: Clip 'n' Save

*A Handy Chart for Aspiring Novelists
(Or, How to Get a Cozy Review)*

Plot: No.
Cryptic dialogue: Yes.
Cryptic dialogue hinting at a dark past betrayal: Yes.
Was it incest?: Probably.
Female character as empowered victim: Yes.
Graphic but ironic use of violent imagery: Sure.
Healing: Yes, but only at the end.
Humour: No.
Irony: Yes.
Characters who spend most of their time remembering things that happened to them before the book actually started: Yes.
Isn't the concept of an "empowered victim" an oxymoron?: Shhh.

The seagulls were staying close to shore. Seven generations of McGoogles had lived here. Seven generations. Their dreams were etched into the rocks as surely as the lines of time were etched onto her face. She touched the bruise on her cheek.

"That bastard!" said Shane. He lifted the bottle to his lips. He drank. Then he stopped.

"They will be here soon," she said. "They will be coming down Cape Breton Road. Unless we're in Newfoundland."

Shane moved near her. His jeans were blue. His white T-shirt was white. And his eyes were filled with a wild rage. "We do not choose our destiny," he said. "Our destiny chooses us!" He lifted the bottle to his lips and he drank until the endless layers of myth that the media had created echoed into silence. He wiped his hand across his mouth.

"But what does that mean?" she said.

"What?"

"What you just said. 'We do not choose our destiny. Our destiny chooses us.' What does that mean, exactly?"

"Um, I don't know. The writer made me say that. He thought it sounded hip. I guess."

"Kind of pretentious, don't you think? I mean, really, why not say: 'We do not choose our family. Our family chooses us.' Or how about, 'We do not choose the weather. The weather chooses us.'"

"Hey, that's pretty good," he said. "You should be a writer."

"Jesus. I need a drink," she said.

"But *I'm* the recovering alcoholic, remember?

You're the empowered earth mother seeking closure."
"Just pass me the friggin' bottle, all right?"

And so on for another 200 pages or so. At which point, we'll all need a drink.

CHAPTER 11 SUMMARY: WHAT YOU'VE LEARNED SO FAR

Here, in a succinct, three-point summary, is everything you need to know about this chapter:

When deciding on any sort of artistic endeavour, Canadians

A. have an awful lot of choices available, although
B. some of the choices are awful, and
C. Canadian celebrities should wear name tags.

That's pretty much it. However, we would also like to mention one of Canada's biggest cultural exports: comedy. Not really an art form, and rarely entertainment, Canadian comedy is currently undergoing a boom the likes of which hasn't been seen since the great comedy exodus of the mid-1980s, when all the famous and wealthy Canuck comics, like Jim Carrey and Mike Myers, left for the States (though it's more accurate to say they left for the States to *become* famous and wealthy). This comedy boom comes largely courtesy of a specialty cable channel, the appropriately named Comedy Network (motto: "We love your idea so much, we want to give you just enough money so you can't do it properly"); one big whoop-de-do annual festival devoted to comedy (Just For Laughs in Montreal, basically a slightly bigger fringe festival); and a realization from tavern owners across Canada that you can get comedians, sketch troupes and improvisors to work for free on the slow nights.

Here's a tip for getting the most out of your next evening at a comedy club: Sit right up front, near the stage, and every time you hear a joke (which, to be honest, won't be that often), instead of laughing just say, "Hah. I guess that's supposed to be funny." This will get you all sorts of attention, and one of the comedians is sure to ask you your name. Tell him your name is "Hancock Lipschitz," and then sit back and enjoy what happens next. As with a hunting dog thrown into the middle of a chicken coop, the comedic possibilities will prove too much and the comedian's head will physically explode before he has a chance to deliver a punchline. Don't worry, comedians are a dime a dozen in this country, and anyway, if they were really any good, they'd have gone to the States. Right?

12

SOCIAL
VALUES

. . . .

How to Be
as Upstanding as
a Canadian

*I*N THIS exciting, action-packed chapter we will be looking at the underlying social values that unite Canadians from east to west to north, coast to coast to coast, rich and poor alike. (Well, not the *really* rich; they operate by their own rules.) The values we will be discussing form the very foundation of Canadian society, the bedrock beneath the topsoil, the rubber tarp under the patio bricks that sticks out near the edge but is otherwise generally not visible, the paste and mortar, the binder twine and duct tape, the glue, the cement, the glorious papier-mâché that holds this country together!

As a new Canadian, you will need to study these and know them off by heart. This should take, oh, at least a couple of minutes.

AUTHORITY

You have to respect it. Canadians have a deep respect for authority, and they prefer law and order to anarchy and freedom. Why? Because the authorities told them to, that's why.

In the notably thin book *Why We Act Like Canadians,* Pierre Berton cites the Mounties as an example of all that is good and pure and noble about Canada. Stalwarts in scarlet jackets. Strong of jaw and pure of heart! Of *course* Pierre said that. He had no choice. The Mounties have incriminating photographs of him (probably involving a goat or something), so naturally he's going to praise them to high heaven. Which is a shame, because everyone knows that it isn't the Mounties we should be admiring—it's the people at our national spy agency, CSIS (pronounced "csis"). They're the real heroes.

Yes, sir. Noble, brave, cuddly, reliable, dependable: CSIS is the best. And we *swear* we thought that goat was of age. So please, for the love of God, call off your goons.

Whew. Anyway. Just remember to do what you're told. Respect authority, move along when the police tell you to, and—if you're a newspaper tycoon or a two-bit columnist— suck up shamelessly to the Royal Family.

RELIGION

Here's everything you need to know about religion in Canada: when Jesus decided to reveal Himself to Canadians, He chose a Tim Hortons as his venue. True story. It happened in September 1998, in the Cape Breton town of Bras D'Or.

In what became known as the "Miracle of the Doughnuts," an image of Jesus began appearing nightly on the wall outside the Bras D'Or Tim Hortons. Hundreds of faithful flocked to the site (although, in honesty, some of them came for the doughnuts). Stranger still, an image of the late Tim Horton began appearing on windows in the Vatican. No, no. We're just kidding. But the Christ of Tim Hortons was real enough.

There was even a movement launched on the Internet to create the Church of Tim Horton. It wasn't as far-fetched as it sounds. After all, the main elements were already in place:

A. a departed saint (Tim)
B. a chain of churches (both drive-thru and sit-in)
C. a hymn ("You've always got time for salvation!")
D. daily communion (a box of timbits and a double-double)
E. a pilgrimage site (64 Ottawa Street North in Hamilton: the very first Tim Hortons, opened in 1964 and still going strong)
F. its very own Mecca (Moncton, New Brunswick, with more Tim Hortons per capita than any other place in Canada), and, last but not least,
G. a faithful following (Canadians, i.e., a tribe of sugar-dependent, dough-addled caffeine addicts)

Sadly, this ecclesiastical movement seems to have faltered, and Christ Himself has left the building. The miracle ended when the assistant manager at the Bras D'Or shop changed some of the light bulbs outside and the image of Jesus disappeared. Still, it is nice to know that even Our Lord and Saviour gets a craving for a maple glazed now and then. In Canada, it's not religion that is the opiate of the masses—it's doughnuts.

HOBBIES: PLUS ÇA CHANGE...

One of the most popular pastimes in Canada is standing in line. Canadians don't queue, exactly, at least not in the British sense. But nor do they rush forward pell-mell like crazed Italians or rampaging Spaniards. Instead, Canadians will stand, for hours if need be, with their arms crossed, frowning severely. Canadians really enjoy a good wait, if only because it allows them to get terribly peeved without having to do anything about it.

You think we at the HTBAC Institute are exaggerating? Here is a passage from an actual book written by Robert Ernest Vernede, a British travel writer, and published way back in 1911. The book was entitled *The Fair Dominion: A Record of Canadian Impressions*. (Thanks to historian Harry Sanders for alerting us to this passage.)

> The Union railway station at Toronto, when I got there, was a seething mass of people and baggage, with an occasional railway official hidden in the vortex. I spent an hour trying to put a bag into the parcel-room, and after that gave up trying. Canadians are singularly patient in matters of this kind. Laden with heavy bags, they will collect in crowds outside the small window of a parcel-room, and burdened thus will wait there for hours without a murmur, while the youth inside lounges about at his leisure. My temper has frequently been stretched to the limit in Germany when I have had to wait perhaps ten minutes for a penny stamp while the Prussian postal official behind the glass slit curled his moustache in imitation of the Kaiser. I think the methods at that parcel-room in Toronto were even more trying... I

kept coming across the same sort of thing at other places. Calgary... Regina... British Columbia...

That was almost a hundred years ago and nothing has changed. Some of those Canadians are probably *still* in line outside that Union Station window, waiting to be served.

CANADIAN PATRIOTISM: A WELLSPRING OF INSPIRATION

The source of all Canadian patriotism is beer commercials. These commercials, aimed at drunken college students, reiterate an important central fact about Canadians. Namely, that they are Canadian. This is celebrated with shouts of "Woo-hoo" and "Yessss!" whenever these commercial messages are aired at bars or performed live at packed sports stadiums. And no, we are not making this up. We wish we were. But we're not.

This sophisticated sense of self-identity (namely, that as Canadians, Canadians are, in fact, Canadian) is only the tip of the proverbial iceberg. More important still is what Canadians *aren't*: American.

Canadians are not American. This might seem self-evident and, yes, even a tad tautological, but in Canada it remains a central logical construct on a par with Newton's Three Laws of Whatever. Canada, you see, is a seething hotbed of anti-Americanism. Anti-Americanism is at a fever pitch, ever rampant and always present. Make no mistake, Canadians harbour a deep and abiding resentment towards their neighbours to the south.

Now, you may have noticed that Canada is not occupied by the American military and that there are no U.S. Marines patrolling the streets. That's because, whereas the Americans might storm the beaches in Granada or wade into a crossfire in Beruit, they are too scared to face the withering looks of disapproval that would surely be cast their way by Canadians if ever they should try to invade the Great White North. The Canadian "look of disapproval" is a strong deterrent. (Sometimes Canadians will roll their eyes as well, so deep is their hatred for all things American.) "Americans," they will say with a sour frown. And then, in a *highly* disapproving manner, they will shake their heads and go *"tch."* This is the sound of Canadian rancour, this is the sound of Canadian rage unleashed upon the world: *tch*.

The thing to remember is this: If, by some tragic circumstance, you yourself are an American (poor soul), NEVER ADMIT IT! As a new Canadian, you can proudly declare allegiance to any culture you like—except American. If you are from Laos, hold Laotian dances and Laotian music fests. If you are from the Caribbean, stage massive street celebrations. If you are Irish, drink green beer and sport a shamrock, maybe get in a fistfight or two. If you believe in voodoo or animal sacrifices or stoning adulterers, that's fine too. But if you are an American, you must completely disavow your homeland. In fact, you must learn to avert your gaze every time you pass a magazine stand or turn on a television set, if only to avoid the corrosive influence of American culture—a culture that Canadians have fervently rejected. In anecdote, at least.

You see, in the hypersensitivity of today's all-inclusive Canada, American culture is just about the only thing left that Canadians are allowed to mock. Other cultures are off limits, but the Americans are still fair game. You can televise one-hour specials with titles like "Boy, Americans Sure Are Stupid!" and you will be applauded for your efforts. You can condemn Americans outright and never be accused of being a bigot. So carp away!

Handy tip! You can adapt any cultural critique you like, simply by inserting the word "American" into it.

Unacceptable: "If you ask me, people who believe in voodoo are idiots."
Acceptable: "Americans are idiots."

Unacceptable: "Islamic culture is based upon the subjugation of women."
Completely acceptable: "American culture is based upon the subjugation of women."

Utterly unacceptable: "I hate Lithuanians! And the Belgians, too. They're so damn ignorant."
Fully, 100% acceptable: "I hate Americans, they're so ignorant."

Try it out! At your next cocktail party read each of the second statements out loud. No one will blink. Then try making the first statements. Hoo-ha!

THE REASON CANADIANS HATE AMERICANS SO MUCH—AND IT'S A GOOD ONE!

We have already covered weather (i.e., "winter"), but that is not enough. To truly master the art of Canadian conversation, you will need to learn how to complain. About Americans, mainly.

Man oh man, do Canadians love to complain about Americans. Indeed, a recent government survey states that the fourth-most popular pastime in Canada is—and I quote—"complaining about those damn Americans." (This ranks just below "complaining about the weather" (#1), "complaining about the government—and why it isn't doing anything about the weather" (#2), and "just generally complaining" (#3).)

Why do we Canadians hate Americans so much? Is it because the United States sent in their troops and toppled our government? Is it because the CIA assassinated our head of state? We should be so lucky. No. It's far worse than that. The ongoing, long-simmering, deep-running rage that most Canadians direct against Americans is based upon the shocking fact that Americans—*brace yourself!*—don't know very much about Canada. It's horrible. But true.

For example, Canadian exports of halibut last year exceeded the standard set by the Bilateral U.S./Canadian Halibut Accord by a full 23%—but do any Americans know about this? *Nooooo.* In fact, based on an informal sampling of responses, very few Americans are even *aware* of the Bilateral Commission on Halibut Quotas. The fact that we made it up just now is no excuse. It's simply another shocking example of the appalling ignorance that the Americans have when it comes to Canada. And boy, are we mad! Why, we're as mad as a porcupine that's been put in a sack and poked with a stick. If those darn Americans don't smarten up, we'll make another beer commercial. We ain't foolin'. We will. So they better watch it!

FUN AND GAMES WITH CANADIAN NATIONALISTS

The next time a proud Canadian complains about how little Americans know about Canada, ask the aforementioned Canadian a simple question: "What is the capital of New Brunswick?" Be prepared to see their confident demeanour shrivel like a punctured condom.

Go ahead, it's lots of fun! Ask away: "What is the capital of New Brunswick?" And then, as they flail about, making hesitant guesses and trying to come up with the right answer, smile and say, "Those darn Americans, so poorly informed about Canada. Not like us Canadians, eh? We know all about our own country. Yessirree, Bob."

We will bet that not one in ten Canadians knows the correct answer (Moncton) and that those who do are probably from New Brunswick.

Note: If you do happen to be talking to someone from New Brunswick—or anyone from the Maritimes or Newfoundland—here are some alternate questions, guaranteed to cause embarrassed smiles and havering half-guesses: "Manitoba and Winnipeg. Which is the city and which is the province? Is Manitoba the city or is Winnipeg the province? Or are they both cities? Or maybe they're both provinces? Which is which?" Yup, you're sure to stump your Maritime friends with that one. Oh, those darn Americans. So woefully uninformed about Canada. So poorly educated. Not like us, eh?

P.S.: Yes, we know that the capital of New Brunswick is not Moncton. The capital of New Brunswick is Halifax.

CANADIANS: NOT AMERICANS! (SOME EXCEPTIONS APPLY)

So there you have it, the two central axioms of Canadian identity, the mantra and the motto of an entire nation:

A. I. Am. Canadian.
B. I am not American.

Please note the following exception to the rule: Quebec.

Quebec nationalists are, of course, exempt from the "Not American" paradigm. Instead, they are NOT Canadian. In fact, the relationship between English Canadians and the United States is remarkably similar to that between the Québécois *pure laine* and the R.O.C. (Rest of Canada). Just as Canadians are obsessed with the Americans, looking down on them while still feeling threatened (a charming blend of insecurity and arrogance), so too do Québécois nationalists look down on the rest of Canada, with the same blend of threatened insecurity and glib arrogance.

Oh yes, you should also note that the Acadians are NOT Québécois. People from Burlington are NOT Torontonians. Calgarians are NOT from Edmonton. Citizens of Charlottetown are NOT from Summerside. People from Nunavut are NOT from Moose Jaw. People from Moose Jaw are NOT from Moosomin. People from Moosomin are NOT from Chicoutimi. And so on and so forth.

This may sound confusing, but it's not. Just remember to define yourself in terms of negation and you'll do fine. For example: Let's say for some reason you end up in Saskatoon—you know, a clerical error or a plane crash or something. If you then choose to make Saskatoon your home (and here we're assuming some sort of head injury sustained during the crash), you must immediately decide what Saskatoon is NOT. So, when someone asks where you're from, whatever you do, don't say "Saskatoon." Instead, you should reply: "Well, I'm sure as hell not from Regina, that's for damn sure!"

Logic? We Don't Need No Steenkin' Logic!
(Unofficial slogan of Canada)

The flaw in this way of thinking is obvious. Simply put: When you define yourself in terms of negation, you don't actually say anything about who you really are. "I'm not a lumberjack, I don't live in an igloo, I don't eat whale blubber, I don't own a dogsled, I can't make a decent sit-com to save my life, etc., etc."

Imagine introducing your significant other in the same manner. "This is my wife, Mary. She isn't a skydiver." Or "You'll have to meet my new boyfriend. He isn't tall. He isn't dark. And he isn't handsome." Doesn't tell you much about them now, does it? Taken to the national level, you can see how quickly this breaks down into *reductio ad absurdum*. Consider the following attributes associated with Americans and see how far you get by defining Canadians simply by adding "not" to the start of each:

If Americans are: loud, rich, mammals . . .
Then Canadians are . . .

You see the problem.

SOCIALIZING WITH CANADIANS
(IN EVERY SENSE OF THE WORD)

Their fervent anti-American views aside, Canadians are, on the whole, a rather sociable people. And there is nothing they enjoy more than to congregate in large numbers to while away the time. The most popular place for this is in hospital waiting rooms and emergency wards. Canadians like to gather and compare symptoms as the hours, and even the days, tick cheerfully past. Every now and then, someone's appendix will rupture in a comical manner and a nurse, giddy from near-exhaustion, will throw back her head and laugh. Sometimes the staff laugh so loud they start to cry.

A six-month wait to see a specialist? A seven-month wait for cancer treatments? A ten-month wait for a pregnancy check-up? These benefits—and many, many more!—are just a small part of Canada's world-class medicare system. Why, Canada's medicare is the envy of . . . well, of the Americans, we suppose.

The Canadian system is better than that of the U.S.A., something Canadians take great pride in. Remember: In Canada you shouldn't judge something by what it could be or what it *should* be, but rather by what it isn't. And in this case, it clearly ISN'T AS BAD AS THE AMERICAN SYSTEM. Is that great or what? In fact, you will often find Canadian nationalists curled up in a fetal position rocking back and forth, back and forth, repeating to themselves over and over again: "Better than the Americans, better than the Americans."

TPWLT

Canada has made great strides in public health care over the years. Indeed, Canada is at the leading edge of Tobacco Package Warning Label Technology (TPWLT: pronounced "tpwlt"). In Canada, strident warnings and graphic pictures of diseased lungs and blackened tracheas adorn cigarette packages, just as photos of mangled cars and bloated livers adorn bottles of wine, and rotting teeth and close-ups of zits adorn chocolate bar wrappers. (Government agencies in Canada are even now working on warnings about annoying in-laws, a dwindling sex drive, and the possibility of sullen adolescent offspring, to be inserted at the start of wedding vows.)

Tobacco warning labels are very important and have been credited with saving countless lives. Many a hapless consumer has been reaching for a pack of cigarettes when, lo! they have spotted the Government of Canada warning alerting them to the fact that—and you're going to be just as surprised as we were—cigarettes are bad for you. "Wow! Who knew?" says the now-enlightened consumer as they opt instead for a pack of chewing gum or maybe a nickel bag of crack cocaine.

Government warning labels are vital to the health and well-being of Canadians everywhere. For example, the authors of this book were once just about to take turns firing a nail gun at each other's head (in a fun-filled game called "Let's Fire This Nail Gun at Each Other's Head") when one of the aforementioned authors (it was Will) noticed that a government label had been affixed to the aforementioned nail gun (Black & Decker Nail Blaster 2000). It read: DO NOT AIM AT PEOPLE. Well, thank God for warning labels! Without them, we would never have guessed that nail guns were not meant to be fired at human beings. I mean, it didn't end the game or anything, but it was still nice to know. (*Note:* The warning said nothing about yippy little dogs or obnoxious parakeets.)

Just think of the money that Canada's health care system, so weighed down with public funds and government largesse, so rich and amply endowed, will save in long-term care because of the time and money it invests to evaluate—and properly label—the many potentially hazardous elements of everyday life. Time and money well spent, we say! And yes, the day will soon come when every newborn baby in Canada will be affixed with a government-approved label: WARNING! LIFE LEADS TO OLD AGE, ILLNESS AND DEATH.

But don't worry. The label won't be attached with a nail gun or anything.

Canada: Smoke-free and jittery (Quebec: Smooth-tasting tobacco goodness)

The one last hold-out in Canada's drive to be smoke-free and fun-less is Quebec. There is a certain laxness in interpreting laws and regulations in *la belle province*. For example, traffic lights in Quebec are more suggestions than anything else. "You may, perhaps, want to consider stopping now, but if not—" Shrug. It's the same with smoking. A non-smoking sign in Montreal means you do not have to smoke if you don't want to. *Handy tip:* If you ever need to bum a cigarette in Montreal, just go to the nearest non-smoking area. That's where all the smokers will be.

LOOKING FOR VICE? GO NORTH, YOUNG MAN!

Newfoundlanders have sex. Northerners have affairs. The North has been dubbed the Land of the Midnight Sin, and for good reason. The Yukon, for one, has the highest per capita divorce rate in the country, caused by a slightly flexible view of what constitutes fidelity. Not that we're saying Yukoners are promiscuous. No sir. And even if they are, so what? You have to put their unique perspective regarding morality in the proper historical context. It could be a holdover from the days of the gold rush when, as we noted earlier, Dawson City was home to more brothels than any other place in North America. Or it could just be the magic of the Northern Lights. *Tourism motto:* "Visit the Yukon! We'll treat you right, if you know what we mean. Heh heh." Either way, for all you young men and bored women out there, Yukon is the place to be: a beautiful northern wonderland stewing in its own vice and overrun with hot divorcées. And come winter, you'll have six months of darkness . . .

CHARITY

As a Canadian, you will definitely want to chip in and do your part. And why not? Charity is a marvellous invention that allows you to assuage your guilt while still feeling vaguely miserable afterwards.

In Canada, there are two (2) basic forms of charity:

1. buying boxes of chocolate-covered almonds
2. giving coins to people at random on the street

You can see what an efficient system this is, particularly the latter. In Canada, you do NOT save up your spare change and then donate it to a homeless shelter or soup kitchen. That is not the way things are done. It is far more effective to partake in the daily "street theatre" of panhandlers. How it works is, someone you have never met asks you for money. And that's it. That's all there is to it.

Now then, when you are approached—and you will be—there are four options available to you:

1. You can pretend that you do not notice the large, mad rambling man with his hand out asking you for money, and pass by with a grim determination in your step.

2. You can offer emotional support and career advice in lieu of cash ("Get a job, you goddamn bum" being a particularly popular bit of free advice).

3. You can mumble something along the lines of "Sorry, not today" and hurry past with a grim determination in your step.

4. You can cave in like the weak-kneed Canadian you are and hand over some of your hard-earned cash. Why? Because someone asked you to. It's as simple as that. (The Goods and Services Tax operates on much the same principle.)

This is Canada, though, where charity is not a celebration but a sombre Calvinistic duty, so whatever you do—*do not gloat!* Don't fling your change at said panhandler and hoot, "Better you than me, pal!" Nor should you cheerfully remark, "Sure, go ahead, have some of my money. What a remarkably inexpensive way to feel I am Doing Good." Nor should you attempt a high-five with other pedestrians. No victory jigs, no *bwahahahaha* laughs, no taunting said panhandlers with a loonie on a piece of string (it turns out that's illegal). Instead, the entire transaction should be completed in near silence, with a grim resolve. Preferably a grim *Calvinistic* resolve.

That's pretty much it. That's how charity works in Canada. Except at Christmas, when the poor develop an insatiable craving for the canned food that the rest of us have had way at the back of our cupboards all year. ("President's Choice canned yams and unsalted kidney beans. Mmm-mmm. That's good eats!")

There is, however, one other important form of charity,

which operates on a national level and benefits, oh, hundreds of people: the Federal Government's Pension Fund, wherein every dollar donated by an MP earns approximately $782 zillion. That's an excellent return. Do you see what canny investors Canadians are?

Alas, some "people" have had the nerve to criticize this wonderful income-generating plan. Stalwart Alliance MP Deborah Grey, for example, known across the land for her tough stand on propriety and ethical behaviour, has vowed never—*ever*—to take part in such a scheme. She denounced it as an immoral, pork-barrelling cash grab. To illustrate her point, here is an economic summary of Initial Investment vs. Financial Return in the (purely hypothetical!) case of Grey's pension fund:

Total cost to Deborah Grey, MP: $14.82
Total return: Millions!! Millions, I tell you! More money than you could ever need. Piles of money to throw in the air. Money to roll around in. Money to burn! Burn, I tell you!

By this point, the solution to Canada's homeless problem should be self-evident. Why not simply sign each panhandler onto the Federal Pension Fund? Under such a scheme, a loonie and two quarters tossed into a cup would eventually be worth thousands upon thousands of dollars.

Question: But where does this extra money come from?
Answer: Who knows? Who cares? It's free money! Free, I tell you! If we could make every person in Canada an MP, we'd be the richest nation on earth.

So the next time a stranger asks you for spare change, vote them into office instead! Shake their hand and say, "You can count on me in the next election." Once we start sending them to Ottawa, we'll have this whole homeless thing licked for good. Yessir.

CANADA'S ORIGINAL INHABITANTS

(Note to Canadian readers: Feel free to skip this part if it makes you feel uncomfortable)

The original inhabitants of Canada (according to current New Age assumptions) were wily Indians and happy-go-lucky Eskimos. Wily and happy, happy and wily, these innocent peoples frolicked in a land of spiritual attuned-ness, without warfare, without slavery, without trade routes, without profit margins and without political alliances.

As Canada's original inhabitants, the Native people once held dominion over the entire northern half of this vast continent, but through a fortunate convergence of disease, invasion, open warfare, suppressed rebellions and duplicitous government treaties, trespassers from Europe were eventually able to pull the land right out from under them like a tablecloth. This is the First Important Historical Fact about Canada: The country was won via a parlour trick.

Today, Native Canadians live on small parcels of land known as "reserves," where they are to be held until they have been properly assimilated. At least, that was the plan. (We don't mean to question their manners or anything, but Native Canadians really haven't kept up their part of the bargain. I mean, they were supposed to have poetically vanished into the twilight by now, right? Right?)

Canadians have two basic attitudes towards the original inhabitants: New Age silliness and muttered envy.

How do you know which tack you should take? Well, if you studied comparative mythology in college and sport a greying goatee and have a highly refined sense of spiritual gullibility, you would choose the first option. If you studied business administration and now sport polyester neckties and a bad toupée, you would choose the second approach.

Note: The authors of this book had originally intended to examine both of these opposing, yet oddly complementary, approaches to Native Canadians in great detail, but, alas, the New Age version of the Mystical Native at One with the Land is so profoundly saccharine and sentimental that, as potential diabetics, we are not allowed to discuss it on the orders of our doctor.

The more common attitude towards Native Canadians, though often unstated—and an attitude you will need to internalize if you truly wish to blend in—is one of low-level simmering resentment. As in: "Native Canadians are so lucky. They get all these perks from the government. They don't have to pay taxes. They get free reserve housing. What a lucky bunch of people! So fortunate! So blessed! So favoured!" Indeed, how could one not envy them?

Political Extremism in Canada

In spite of the enviable position and splendid advantages they enjoy, Native Canadians will still, on occasion, block a golf course or put logs across a road as a protest over unresolved land claims. In Canada, this marks them as dangerous radicals, on a par with Irish Republicans or Basque terrorists. (*Logs across a road?!* Do you see how dangerous it is to live in the Great White North? Don't say we didn't warn you.)

If you want to come to Canada, you will have to be brave. And if—heaven forbid—some violent, wild-eyed activist goes so far as to BLOCK A ROAD, you should take a deep breath, fight back your fear and find a detour. (You should then immediately pen a letter to your local newspaper about how commuters—the bread and butter of Canadian society—are being held "hostage.")

Having to deal with road-blocking radicals is the type of supreme sacrifice that you, as a Canadian, will be asked to make. It's a heavy price to pay for half a continent, but it's one that most Canadians are willing to make.

In fact, Canada is a veritable hotbed of political extremism. The motto of Native Canadian hardliners seems to be: "You stole our land, destroyed our culture, killed all the buffalo, introduced infectious diseases, took our children away, banned our language and shattered our society. If you don't watch out, any day now we're going to get angry! I mean, we were angry before, but we're going to get *really* angry. Why, we might even block another road! You'll have to take the long way around to get home—then you'll be sorry."

In Quebec, meanwhile, the weapon of choice is a referendum. The separatist motto? "Back off, Jack, or we'll hold a plebiscite!" After all, Native or non-Native, Aboriginal or non-Aboriginal, French or English, there is only so far you can push a Canadian.

POP QUIZ

Question: How do you get two hundred drunken Canadians out of a swimming pool?

Answer: You say, "Excuse me, could you please get out of the pool?"

This is an old joke, much beloved by Canadians because it reflects well upon their non-confrontational manner. For example, when the members of APEC (Association of Third-World Dictators) met for a chinwag in Vancouver a few years ago, the police were asked to clear a route through student protestors to make room for the dignitaries' motorcade. "Just roll over them! *Roll over them with tanks!!*" the Chinese delegates had jokingly suggested. At least, we think they were joking.

Send in the tanks? No. That wasn't the Canadian Way. (And besides which, the tanks—being Canadian—probably wouldn't have started.) Instead, just as in the quip quoted earlier, the red-coated stalwarts of the Royal Canadian Mounted Police (*see* All-time favourite Canadian archetypes) politely asked the protestors to move along. "Excuse me, could you please get out of the pool?". . . and then they blasted 'em with pepper spray. What a great sight gag! And another example of the wonderful sense of humour with which Canadians are blessed.

POP QUIZ (revised)

Question: How do you get two hundred Canadians out of a swimming pool?

Answer: Declare the War Measures Act. Send in the troops. Fire tear-gas canisters directly into the crowds. Pepper-spray protestors at random. Arrest and detain people without bail. Hold them overnight in a prison cell—the colder the better. Make them strip. Stick your fingers into their bodily orifices. Open their mail, tap their phones and then, when they complain, club 'em again! The fun never ends in Canada, the Peaceable Kingdom.

CHAPTER 12 SUMMARY: WHAT YOU'VE LEARNED SO FAR

Canadians confuse conformity with politeness. They hate Americans, but they're not really sure why. And, unless forced to do so, they don't like thinking about Native issues or poor people. There, in a nutshell, are the three most distinguishing ethical and moral characteristics of Canadians.

Now, before we move on to our next chapter, we have a couple of things to clear up. First off, it turns out that Deborah Grey has decided to opt back into her pension fund. We regret our error. Turns out she's not any more honourable than the next politician. What a shocker.

Also, a word of warning regarding the section on charity. If you're walking down St. George Street in Toronto or strolling through the Old Strathcona neighbourhood in Edmonton,* you might want to be careful about giving money to weirdly dressed, bearded men who stumble towards you talking to themselves loudly. Sure, they might be homeless, but they're just as likely to be fully tenured philosophy professors from the nearby university. Why take that chance? Don't make eye contact, and try not to let the smell of musty ideas and mouldering irrelevance get to you.

---

* This advice also applies for the Broadway district in Saskatoon, Ste. Catherine in Montreal, the hill in Fredericton and almost anywhere you go in Victoria.

IMPORTS, EXPORTS AND ESCORTS

. . . .

How to Make Money
Like a Canadian (or not)

*I*N THIS chapter you will learn how to *import* knowledge (by choosing the right university) and how to *export* your skills (by choosing the correct career path—defined as "the one least likely to cripple you")—to best suit Canada's economic system (pyramid schemes and coffee punch-cards) in order to purchase goods and services, such as those provided by *escorts*. Ultimately, it's all about sex. Though we mention the word *sex* merely as a ploy to keep your attention.

CHOOSING THE RIGHT UNIVERSITY: THE KEY TO SUCCESS!

As any reputable doctor will tell you, the secret to a healthy life in Canada is to pick your parents well. If your parents are financially secure, reasonably attractive and in fairly good health, with straight teeth and no incipient mental illness, well, congratulations. You've won the gene-pool lottery. You are probably reasonably attractive yourself and have a fairly decent chance at a longer-than-average life expectancy. Unless you smoke or drink too much. Or move to Sudbury. Anyway, aside from a few minor environmental influences, you're probably going to have a pretty good life. If you can find a job. (You're going to have to pay for all those cigarettes somehow.*)

There are a lot of jobs out there, but many of them involve heavy lifting, "customer service skills" and/or mops. To get a plum position with a good maximum-income-to-minimum-effort ratio, you will need a university degree. Fortunately, thanks to constantly falling educational standards and a recent phenomenon known as "creeping grade inflation," getting an undergraduate degree today doesn't have to take that much elbow grease. What it does take is money. And lots of it.

With postgraduate educational standards at an all-time low, the cost of going to college or university is at an all-time high. Which, of course, clearly contradicts both the Malthusian Law of Supply and Demand and John Kenneth Galbraith's advanced theory about proprietary quality and provisional quantity. (We rooted around in the thesaurus, used the spell-checker on the big words, and we still don't have a clue what that previous sentence means. Which is another reason you need to go to college or university. So you can learn how to use a computer program that will look up big words and spell them for you.)

To fund a picaresque journey through the halls of academe, you will need either A. wealthy parents (see above), or B. a subsistence-level student loan that barely covers the cost of beer and cigarettes, let alone textbooks. The key is to *invest* your student loan in something lucrative, like

---

* And they aren't just giving that beer away free, you know.

a dot.com empire or an MPs' pension fund, and then simply live off the return. Personally, we invested our student loans in empties—and we must say it paid off handsomely.

So, you can see how important it is to get a higher education. And when we say "higher," we are not speaking figuratively. Any parents out there can rest assured that the campuses of this great land are every bit as riddled with potheads and dope fiends as they ever were. Take a walk through a dorm anywhere in Canada and inhale deeply. That's the smell of hard work wafting through the hallways.

But how to choose which college or university is the right one for you? Which temple of academic excellence, which elevated educational institution, which intellectually insouciant ivory tower will set you on the path to success? (See how much fun you can have once you learn to use a computer's thesaurus?)

You could go out and spend $16.95 on the *Maclean's Guide to Canadian Universities & Colleges* ("Whither Higher Education?"), but why? That's a ridiculous amount of money to spend on a magazine, especially when you've just purchased this entire book for the much more reasonable sum of $19.95.

Besides, we've already bought the damn magazine, and we can tell you right now that the people over at *Maclean's* missed a few things. For starters, they criticized York University for having few services for the students who live in residence. Well, we happen to know that there's a plethora of pubs and strip bars in North York all conveniently located near the campus, some within walking distance. How could the investigative geniuses at *Maclean's* have missed that?

Here, then, is the Official HTBAC Step-by-Step Guide to Higher Education in Canada.

Step 1: Buy the *Maclean's Guide to Canadian Universities & Colleges*.

Step 2: Ignore the stuff in the *Maclean's* guide about the number of doctoral candidates on staff and about class size and the number of books available in the library and any other irrelevant information.

Step 3: Learn to read between the lines. When you're reading the listings, look for the important stuff. For example:

- Best female-to-male ratio: University of Victoria
- Best male-to-female ratio: Carleton University in Ottawa
- Best nightlife available on campus: St. Francis Xavier, home of the X-men and all things X-rated. (Runner-up: Lakehead University in Thunder Bay; there isn't any nightlife available in town, so the campus is your only option.)
- Best nightlife available off campus: McGill University in Montreal, where the pagan fleshpots of Sherbrooke and Ste. Catharine are within stumbling distance of your classroom and/or residence. (Runners-up: University of Toronto, located between Bloor and College, where a wide range of diversions are available; University of Alberta, steps away from Edmonton's Old Strathcona neighbourhood, which is exactly like Bloor Street, only as a 1/100th-scale model.)
- Least nightlife available either on campus or off: Brandon University, in a city where they really do turn the traffic lights off at night. (Runner-up: University of Victoria. Don't let them lie to you. Sipping cappuc-

cino while sitting cross-legged on the sidewalk begging for change is not an activity, much less a recreation. Besides, the seniors complain if you make too much noise after 9:00 P.M.)

- Most attractive campus: University of Saskatchewan in Saskatoon with its riverside setting and sandstone buildings.

- Least attractive campus: York University, deep in the remote tundra north of Toronto. According to campus myth, York was originally designed to be built in southern California, where the wind-tunnel effect created by the concrete towers would help draw cooling Pacific breezes inland. Now, as you may have noticed, Toronto isn't exactly situated on the Pacific Ocean. Instead, they ended up with a campus that has a constant wind chill warning in effect, even during the hottest days of summer. York is an example of what happens when architects go bad and concrete is on sale.* (Runners-up: University of Regina, where the architects made the mistake of designing the campus to match the style of the surrounding community; Calgary's Mount Royal College, which looks like a cheap set for a bad 1970s science-fiction series.)

- Most hidden campus: University of Lethbridge, which is tucked out of sight against a hillside in the badlands. You enter on the top floor and then descend as you move through the building. (Runner up: George Brown

---

* Both Will and Ian attended York University, and as such they have, how shall we say, "mixed" feelings about the place. Meaning they loathed it and yet they also vehemently disliked it. They hated it and, at the same time, they despised it. You know, complicated, ambivalent emotions.

College in Toronto, which is scattered all over the city, much like a pizza chain that wants an outlet in every possible neighbourhood.)

Note: Although the *Maclean's* guide was very helpful, as a coaster if nothing else, Will and Ian also relied on their own extensive personal knowledge when it came to evaluating the universities and colleges listed above. Especially York. (School motto: "On strike since 1987!")

Step 4: The final and most important step. Toss out the *Maclean's* guide and make your decision based on the following criteria: Do you want to go to the university or college in your own hometown, thus allowing you to live with your parents rent-free, thereby leaving you with lots of disposable income for things like beer and birth control and zip-lock bags full of oregano? ("Honest, Mom. It's for spaghetti sauce.") Or do you want to go to university somewhere really, really, really far away from your family, so that you can get into all kinds of trouble, even though you won't have as much money to buy beer with—but where you may actually get to use your birth control?

Remember, the point of going to university is to have a little fun while you're still young enough to recover the next morning. That's why all the early-morning classes are taught by graduate students. Hey, don't worry. They're hungover too.

Once you get your degree (and, quite frankly, you'd have to screw up really badly not to graduate), it's off into the real world, where you will have to get a "job," which will occasionally require something called "working." For this, you will be paid "money," which (according to John Kenneth Galbraith) can be used to purchase transactional goods. Like beer. Or birth control. Or back issues of *Maclean's*.

OCCUPATIONAL HAZARDS

You went out and got yourself an education. You invested your student loan wisely and are now heavily in debt. The next stage? Avoiding work.

To help you select the best jobs to avoid, we have compiled a list of potential dangers and disabilities associated with certain Canadian occupations. These are real maladies, as reported in the *Atlas of Occupational Markers in Human Remains* and the *Journal of the American Medical Association*.

Hooker's elbow: No, it's not what you think. Hooker's elbow is a bone spur common among ice fishermen, the Inuit in particular, caused by the constant yanking of a line while standing stationary. The world's original repetitive strain injury.

Musher's knee: A bone deformation caused by pushing off on a dogsled using the same leg again and again.

Snowmobiler's back: Damage to one's vertebrae caused by the constant vibration of the machine and the hunched posture of the driver.

Paddler's toe: A deformation of foot joints that plagues long-distance canoeists, first noted among voyageurs in the 1700s. (Mind you, there aren't a lot of job openings today for "voyageurs," so you probably won't run into this.)

Beer-drinker's finger: A swelling in the finger, sometimes accompanied by bruising and lacerations, caused by the repeated opening of beer tabs. (Switching to twist-offs doesn't help either, because all you're doing is swapping one malady for another.) Again, this is a real affliction. We kid you not.

Mal de raquette: Stress and chronic pain in the knees and hips caused by wearing snowshoes.

Humper's lump: A strain or even outright dislocation of the lower neck that afflicts lumberjacks and lumber carriers. (Not to mention "Squashed Lumberjack Syndrome," an all-too-common affliction, usually fatal.)

So: as long as you manage to avoid becoming a professional lumberjack, ice fisherman or dogsled operator, you should do fine.

CONGEALED CASH: THE GENIUS OF THE CANADIAN PUNCH-CARD SYSTEM

If humping and hooking and mushing are out, what is the preferred approach to gainful employment? Let's start at the beginning . . . "So I'm at this cocktail party, right? And Margaret Atwood is there, and she can't keep her hands off me." No, that's not what we meant. Let's look at the very basis of the Canadian economy. How is wealth generated? How does the private sector work? What is the foundation of Canadian monetary theory? And what's with all these questions?

Well, after an in-depth, extensive survey of Canadian economics, we at the HTBAC Institute have come to the conclusion that the primary form of business transaction in Canada is that of the "customer loyalty" punch-card. These act as concentrated—or congealed—cash, to be used in lieu of real currency. In Canada, true wealth lies in the size of one's punch-card collection. Canadians carry around thick wads of these cards. Wallets and purses are bulging to the breaking point—and no wonder. By using this cost-effective method of accumulated discounts, you can—after spending just $48.90 on coffee—get as much as 7% off the price of your next regular non-flavoured standard cup. Punch in five more cups and you get a free latte. Punch in fifty, and you get really jittery.

Video rentals work the same way. Cinemas, bakeries and airlines: ditto. Sooner or later, every business in Canada will have its own system of punch-cards: divorce lawyers, funeral homes, sperm banks, even elected representatives. It all adds up! Kidney transplant recipients are already being issued punch-cards with little pictures of kidneys on them. And hey, the fourth kidney is free.

Handy tip! You can cut costs considerably by purchasing your own personal hole punch. Just grab a handful of cards at the shop of your choice and start punchin' away! *Note:* It's best not to do this right at the counter. The clerks tend to get upset, for some reason, so be discreet. "Let's see, I'll have a . . ." (turns away for a moment) *chunka-chunka-chunka-chunka* "tall mochachinno with . . ." *chunka-chunka* "extra froth" *chunka* "for free."

CANADA: A HAVEN FOR TELEMARKETERS AND PYRAMID SCHEMES

But how do you earn the income to purchase the merchandise to get the punch-cards? Simple: telemarketing pyramid schemes.

A survey of recent telephone activity here at the Institute revealed the following. On an average day, 87% of calls received by Canadians come from A. bill collectors,

B. wrong numbers, C. someone trying to flog time-share vacation properties in the Muskokas, D. people offering a great! new! way! to! save! money! on long-distance phone calls, E. angry editors demanding to know where the last rewrites are, F. people selling cheap hydroelectric power, and G. people selling bulk meat.

Seriously. We're not making up the bulk meat thing. Apparently, this is the latest craze. A couple of families will go in together and buy a cow. It's a good thing we at the Institute have tremendous willpower, or we'd be sitting at home right now, incommunicado, surrounded by freezers full of Alberta beef and Ontario pork (or Brazilian beef and British lamb, as the case may be), all of which would be slowly thawing due to the latest power outage triggered by whichever fly-by-night power company had the good fortune to unleash their smoothest-voiced telemarketer on us. Which is just another example of—hang on, that's the phone . . .

The point is: If you answer your telephone in Canada and it doesn't end up costing you any money, you're ahead of the game. (And don't forget the punch-card. Your seventh cow is free!)

Based on this research, we conclude that the single best business to launch in Canada would be a telemarketing pyramid scheme where you mail a cow to every second person on a list provided by time-share condo salesmen in the Muskokas—all the better to save you money on long-distance phone calls. To angry editors.

INVESTING IN CANADIAN COMPANIES (IT'S ALL ABOUT SEX)

Canadians may not have much sex—at least, not once they graduate from college—but Canadian companies have *sex appeal*. And while power may be the ultimate aphrodisiac, watching your stock portfolio grow is certainly a close second.

Why work for your money when your money can work for you? As a student, you may have invested your government loan and reaped the benefits of debt and penury. Well, now it is time to get serious. But what to buy? What to sell? And what the heck does TSE stand for anyway? (Toronto Stock Exchange.) How about NASDAQ? (Nobody knows.) Anyone who has opened a newspaper to the financial section has been stymied by the complex and arcane nature of stock listings. What's going up, what's going down, what should you hoard, what should you fob off on other, less astute investors than yourself? It's very complicated. The listings are harder to figure out than a racing form—which is a fairly good comparison, actually.

Think of investing in the markets as though you were going to the track. You're taking a calculated risk, and the trick is not to wager any of the money you need to cover the essentials of life (beer, cigarettes, insulin, shelter, humour books by Canadian authors, etc.). Instead, you should only play what you can afford to lose (who needs shelter, really?). Sure, you could study the stats, playing the thoroughbreds or betting on the trotters by how well they run on a muddy track in a month that ends in "r." But what's the point? You might just as well bet on a horse with a cute name. Remember: You're gambling, and any attempt to apply scientific theory to the experience will only take the fun out of it.

Same thing with the stock market. Only difference is, instead of picking a company with a cute name, you should invest according to one simple criterion: Sex. That's right, the company you choose has to have sex appeal. Or, even better, SEX appeal.

Take a company like Bombardier. They're a *femme fatale*. Very French, very mysterious. You can imagine them breaking your heart over a croissant and a cup of coffee. You'll never really know them, but for as long as you're involved, you'll be constantly surprised by the things they do. (Like using government grants to buy out a rival German company in order to sell subway cars to Peru. See how exotic they are?) If Bombardier were a woman, it would be Genevieve Bujold.

Or take a company like Canadian Tire. Sex appeal? Certainly. In that rugged, sturdy, not-too-flashy Canadian way. Imagine actor Paul Gross in full Mountie regalia. Sexy, sure, but comfortable and reliable first and foremost. You can count on Canadian Tire to deliver the goods, and they're not going to do anything too surprising. No whips or harnesses in bed, no sudden dabblings in alternative lifestyles. (And if they do try to move to the States, they'll quickly see the error of their ways and return home without losing too much of your hard-earned money.)

If you're looking for a riskier investment, you might want to consider a company like Nortel, the Pamela Anderson of Canadian businesses. Puffed up, pouty, artificially enhanced and willing to do almost anything to attract your attention (and your money). You'll have fun, but you'll probably regret it in the morning when she runs off with a skinny-armed, tattooed rocker, leaving you behind holding the bag. That's Nortel in a nutshell.

Bre-X was like Margot Kidder (fabulously entertaining until the breakdown), Rogers Cable is like Alanis Morissette (you can't escape them), and Alcan is like Tom Green, more disgusting than funny, more vulgar than charming, constantly polluting the environment—and yet still somehow able to bag the babes (or government subsidies, as the case may be).

See how easy investing becomes? You simply pick a company according to your sexual preferences and appetites, buy a little stock, invest a little capital, set up a small portfolio—and soon you'll go be going broke just like everyone else. But you'll have had more fun. And by fun, we mean, of course. . . sex.

HOW TO FILL OUT A GRANT APPLICATION FORM

You now know the key to success (either a good university or wealthy parents). You've learned what drives the economy (punch-cards and pyramid schemes) and how to invest (by sexual preference). But the essential skill you will need, if you are to achieve your goals of economic well-being and happiness—or, failing that, a fat bloated bank account—is this: You will need to know how to fill out a grant application form. Whether you run a laboratory or a small business or a sprawling multi-limbed corporation or even your own personal think-tank, you will need to know how to apply for government assistance.

It has been estimated (just off the top of our heads) that businesses in Canada spend approximately 50% of their time filling out increasingly incoherent tax forms and the remaining 50% applying for government grants and tax subsidies. It seems to us that it would be easier to let the businesses keep the damn GST in the first place, but what do we know?

Government grants are the source of all private wealth in Canada. How it works is, you get a grant application form (that's the first step) and then you fill it in (that's the second step). Simple, no?

Successful recent submissions include the following:

- "Employee Empowerment: Pushing the Envelope outside the Box—in a Proactive Manner."
- "A Study of the Effects of Sunlight on Exposed Skin in Florida at Spring Break." (Submitted by a forum of suspiciously well tanned research assistants.)
- "Make Money Quick! A Guide to Filling Out Grant Application Forms."
- "Profit Margins? Ha! Who Needs Profit Margins? Let's Sell Everything on Consignment!" (A study of the Canadian publishing industry.)
- "Federalist Oppression: How the Government of Canada Has Relentlessly and Heartlessly Debased Québécois Culture since Time Immemorial." (An application for federal assistance, from the Artists' Collective Sovereignty Co-op of Quebec. "We spit on you, you pig-dog federalists. We spit on you! Now give us some money.")

Finally, a farmer in southern Saskatchewan was recently given a $12-million grant for his avant-garde, site-specific art project "Crop Rotation: A Work in Progress." (The authors of this book would have interviewed the farmer-artist firsthand, if only he'd been able to stop giggling.)

CHAPTER 13 SUMMARY: WHAT YOU'VE LEARNED SO FAR

Money is good. It can help you get beer. And beer can help you get sex. Or at least it can help you better *enjoy* sex. It is also important to study hard and get a good education, and if you can have some sex while you're doing it, that's even better. The stock market is a scam. Unless you think of it like sex. And that's it. That is the sum total of wisdom contained within this chapter. Oh, and one other thing. You know that John Kenneth Galbraith bit? Proprietary quality and provisional quantity? We made that up.

HOW THE CANADIAN GOVERNMENT WORKS

. . . .

It doesn't.

PROGRESSIVE CONSERVATIVES, RESPONSIBLE GOVERNMENT AND OTHER OXYMORONS

. . . .

How to Rule Like a Canadian

*D*o you remember back near the beginning of this book, when we described Ottawa as a semi-tropical paradise? We were lying. Ottawa may be semi-retired and semi-conscious, but semi-tropical it ain't. It's no paradise, either. (Actual civic motto: "Ottawa: Technically Beautiful." How's that for a ringin' endorsement?) Ottawa, you see, is full of bureaucrats, and bureaucrats are full of themselves.

Bureaucrats are to Ottawa what gunslingers were to the American West: the definitive archetypal figure. In Canada, it is the Lone Bureaucrat who strikes fear and awe into the hearts of timid townsfolk. And so he should. Canadians write a mean memo. This is the Land of the Bureaucrat.

The secret to having a good time in Ottawa? Move.

No, we aren't knocking Ottawa as a city. It's an attractive enough place with lots of green space, and it routinely ranks high on the list of cities to raise a family in. But

Ottawa is also, well, Ottawa. And as such, it is crawling with humourless government aides. And as if that weren't bad enough, you've got yer backbenchers roamin' about with impunity as well. Now, we're not suggesting that the silly-twit chromosome is especially high amongst back-benchers, because our lawyers warned us about doing that again, but there is something about the combination of self-importance and impotent anonymity that makes back-benchers particularly petty. Take Liberal MP Tom Wap-pel, who all but spit upon an eighty-year-old blind war vet merely because the man hadn't voted for him in the—hang on a sec, our lawyers are on the line.

CANADIAN DEMOCRACY: IT'S ALL ABOUT CHOICE!

At some point as a Canadian, you will be expected to vote. Federal elections in Canada are held every two or three months, and at those times you will be asked to trudge down to your neighbourhood high school gymnasium and do your bit to keep the wheels of democracy turning.

In Canada, political allegiance is not about "ideology" or "party lines" or "principles." It's about choosing your side and then sticking with 'em, through right or wrong, thick or thin. Unless, of course, you voted Alliance, in which case the correct response is to FLEE! FLEE FOR YOUR LIVES!

Here are your choices, such as they are:

The Liberals

Some parties have platforms. The Liberals have public opinion polls. Some parties have heart. The Liberals have a weathervane where their heart would normally be. The Tin Woodsmen of Canadian politics, that's the Liberals. They're as slippery as greased eels, and as hard to pin down as Jell-O to a wall. And, this being Canada, they have been rewarded for their behaviour with three successive majority governments—and counting.

How slimy are the Liberals? Here's just one example: In the 1993 election, their Red Book policy declared that the Liberals would allow for an independent Ethics Counsellor—as opposed to one appointed by and beholden to the Prime Minister Himself. They swore they would do this. It was part of the Official Liberal Policy. (We can hear the chortling of jaded Canadian voters even as we write.)

Fast-forward to 2001: The Official Opposition—frustrated at the way the Liberals are hemming and hawing and stalling and stonewalling over allegations of bank loans, golf courses and apparent conflicts of interest—introduces a motion in the House of Commons taken *directly* from the Liberal Party's Red Book. Citing the Liberals' very own policies, the Opposition moves that the government keep its promise and create an independent Ethics Counsellor. The motion even quotes, verbatim, sections of the Red Book itself. The result? The Liberals vote against their own policy and defeat the motion 145 to 122. How upstanding! How admirable! How Liberal. (Memo to Liberal backbenchers: Two words—"baaa" and "baaa.")

The Liberals also promised to rescind the Free Trade Agreement with the U.S. and to abolish the GST. Of course, when they said "rescind," they meant "expand." And when they said "abolish," they meant "roll naked in a pit of money like Scrooge McDuck on crack cocaine, laughing hysterically all the while."

The Liberal Party is in power. Forever. So get used to it. Great Liberal prime ministers of the past include: John Turner.

The Progressive Conservatives

The Conservatives used to be a political party. Now they're this bizarre fringe group that walks around wild-eyed like a crazed street person insisting to anyone who will listen, "We're a national alternative. We're a national alternative." This is the party that gave us Brian Mulroney. 'Nuff said. The party's name itself represents the ultimate in Canadian political nomenclature: Progressive Conservative. Not unlike the "Forward-Backward Party" or the "Pushme-Pullme Party." Which is apt. The federal Tories have all the unerring political instincts of lobotomized gnats. And did we mention that whole Brian Mulroney thing?

Great Conservative prime ministers of the past include: John Abbott, Arthur Meighen and Kim Campbell.

The Canadian Alliance (name change pending)

Unlike the Liberals, the Alliance actually believes in something. Unfortunately, what they believe in is capital punishment, public humiliation of their own leaders and arming unborn babies. ("If every unborn child was given its own handgun, there would be no more abortions!")

> *Question:* They oppose abortion *and* support capital punishment?
> *Answer:* Yes.
> *Question:* What are they, a bunch of idiots?
> *Answer:* Apparently.

The Alliance Party supports think-tank studies such as "Asian Immigrants: Threat or Menace?" and they use outdated, old-fashioned words like "sodomite," "Christian morality" and "political accountability." The Alliance believes in grass-roots democracy. The Liberals believe in greased-palm bureaucracy. The choice is yours.

The NDP

The NDP are about as fashionable as permed hair and disco sideburns. As Canada's national socialist party fades into the twilight of its increasingly irrelevant ideology, many a media pundit gets nostalgic and speaks wistfully about a possible "retro craze" that will see the silliness that is socialism taken seriously again by someone outside of the CBC. ("Coming up Next on *Counterspin:* International Trade—Threat or Menace?") The NDP believes in massive government intervention at every level of your life, from the bedroom to the boardroom. Living under an NDP government would be like renting a room from your parents. "Honey, don't you think you've been using too much hot water?" "Where are you going?" "When will you be back?" "Your father and I worry about you."

Party motto: "Vote NDP, because more red tape is just what this country needs!"

> *Question:* They oppose capital punishment but they *support* abortion?
> *Answer:* Yes.
> *Question:* What are they, a bunch of idiots?
> *Answer:* Apparently.

There are now more members of the Rankin Family than there are card-carrying members of the NDP.

The Natural Law Party

A party run by Yogic flyers, Natural Law promises levitation lessons and mystical meditation for the masses. Which is to say, of all the parties in Canada, Natural Law makes the *least*-outrageous promises. (The odds are better that you will see levitating MPs on Parliament Hill than that you will see an independent Ethics Counsellor.)

The Radical Middle and One-Winged Birds:
Thinking Like a Canadian

We are in the extreme centre, the radical middle.
That is our position.
—*Pierre Trudeau explains the Liberal Party's stance*

In Canada, to be successful in politics, you must be prepared to blaze a death-defying trail to the middle of the road—any road. If you are right-wing, you must reassure voters that you will protect medicare and social spending. If you are left-wing, you must be committed to fiscal responsibility and a balanced budget.

Here is an actual quote from an actual Canadian leader—Joe Clark, who was PM back in the late seventies and early eighties.

> When I was a boy in High River, Alberta, I used to lie in the fields and study the heavens. And I noticed a very peculiar thing about birds. They have two wings, a left wing and a right wing. And if they had only one wing, they would fly around in circles.

No, Joe. If a bird has only one wing, it doesn't fly in circles—it plummets to the earth. What exactly were you smoking back when you were lying in the fields staring at the sky?

The Bloc Québécois

Sigh. Only in Canada. A federal separatist party. Talk about a contradiction in terms. Stranger still, in the mid-nineties, the separatists were, are you ready for it, "Her Majesty's Loyal Opposition."

And there you have it: the vast smorgasbord of choice, the electoral lunch-special buffet that is the Canadian political system. You may want to lie down a while with a cold cloth on your forehead, so overcome by the dizzying range as you must surely be.

THE OFFICE OF THE PRIME MINISTER

In the United States, presidents are removed from office by A. assassination, B. scandal, or C. scandal *followed* by assassination.

In Canada, the prime minister is removed only when they begin to smell bad. And is it just me, or has anyone else noticed a pungent aroma wafting from the PM's office lately? Someone should really go check to see if he's still alive.

The most popular pastime of Canadian leaders is announcing their retirement. There is nothing Canadian politicians enjoy more than giving a good farewell speech before stepping down and then walking away, into the sunset... only to come bounding back on stage like an actress trying to squeeze one more ovation from the audience.

Canadian politicians are like mythical beasts. You have to kill them three times before they stay down. No fewer than four of Canada's last six PMs retired—only to stage a comeback. Joe Clark, John Turner, Pierre Trudeau, Jean Chrétien: each was pronounced DOA only to come lumbering back to life. Election day in Canada has become a night of the living dead.

HOUSES: UPPER AND LOWER

There are two parliamentary houses in Canada. The House of Commons is an elected body whose members are entrusted with maintaining the dignity and decorum of Canadian parliamentary democracy. They do this by openly questioning the dignity and decorum of the other members at every opportunity. They also enjoy yelling witticisms at each other. Such as "Shut up!", "Sit down!" or, for a change of pace, "Shut up and sit down!" That sort of thing. It's very dignified.

Canada's upper house is the Senate. The main role of the Senate is justifying its own existence. Standard Senate speech: "Why the Senate Is Important."

THE QUEEN

Canada is a democratic society based upon the ideals of equality and opportunity for all. The symbol of this democracy is an unelected member of a foreign royal family whose status is determined purely by bloodline and an in-bred, outdated hereditary class system. You know, sometimes the satire writes itself . . .

THE CONSTITUTION OF CANADA

(The most exciting topic in the history of the universe!)

There is nothing Canadians enjoy more than to get together and have a heated debate about their Constitution. This, in turn, leads to the second-most-popular political activity in Canada: holding referendums.

Canada! "United we stand. Divided, we somehow manage to muddle through."

How to Draft a Referendum Question

Clarity, that's the key. For example, you can't simply ask:
"Do you want to break away from Canada, completely and
utterly: yes or no?" Instead, you have to cover every possible contingency. Here is an example of the correct way to
present a referendum question:

> The Province of Quebec, after consulting the tarot
> cards and having examined intently the intestines of
> sheep, has decided to pursue a non-retroactive part-
> nership proposal with Canada inclusive of—but not
> limited to—the commonly accepted notion of a sov-
> ereign nation, but still with our Canadian passports
> and our cozy transfer payments from Ottawa. Do you
> agree to disagree with this proposed proposal or do
> you reject rejecting it at this time? Check only one:

> YES: I do not want to not accept a rejection of this
>   proposal
> NO: I *do* want to not accept a proposed rejection of
>   the accepted proposal

How to Reject a Referendum Ballot

Boy, did Canadians ever get a kick out of those dumb
Americans and their ham-handed attempts in 2000 at trying to make sure every vote in the crucial state of Florida
was counted. Ha! What a joke.

In a rare moment of cross-border cooperation, we here
at the HTBAC Institute have developed a primer for our

American cousins on how to properly reject a ballot. In the 1995 Quebec referendum, thousands of pro-Canada *non* votes were rejected out of hand—and rightly so! Quebec's PQ ballot-counters, trained to discern the true intent of voters, were able to bypass any silly American notions of "public scrutiny." So a few Anglos objected, so what? Anglos in Quebec are always upset about something. The main thing is that the spirit of democracy was upheld.

Here, then, is a handy guide to evaluating ballots, as provided by Quebec's Chief Elections Officer (who was, naturally, appointed for life by the Parti Québécois).

 Intent: *oui*. (Clearly, the voter is saying, "I reject voting *non*.")

 Intent: *oui*. (The check mark could easily mean, "*Oui!* I agree to NOT vote *non*.")

 Intent is not clear.

 Ballot rejected. Voter marked outside of the box, therefore, intent is not clear.

OUI

Clearly the voter intended to vote *oui*. Why else would they have left it blank?

REVEALED AT LAST: THE (REAL) SECRET
TO WIELDING POWER IN CANADA

By now, your political appetite has undoubtedly been whetted. Have you developed a thirst for power? A craving for status? Not a problem. So you want to be prime minister, eh? You want to be the omnipotent master of the Great White North. There's no shame in that. It's only natural to be engulfed by ambition when you see the type of leaders Canada produces. Come on. Any country that can elect Jean Chrétien three times in a row is a country ripe for conquering. You want to take over? Don't apologize. It's an understandable craving. You are, after all, still new at being a Canadian. You still have raw ambition and a burning passion to change things. Don't worry, that will pass as time goes by.

You will eventually adapt to the Canadian milieu, but in the meantime, we at the HTBAC Institute have produced a Top Secret Document outlining the key to wielding power in Canada. Think "magician." Think "misdirection." Think "boredom."

To begin with, let us play a game: The people are up in arms. The Parliament Buildings are up in flames. The police are out of control. French-Canadian nationalism is boiling over. A billion-dollar oil rig topples into the sea. Your Armed Forces have beaten some poor kid to death. Your trusted Cabinet is corrupt and the Senators are asleep (as per usual). The economy is caught in an upward-downward-expanding-contracting-progressive-conservative period of adjustment. The wolves are at the door and the Americans want the next dance.

The nation turns its desperate gaze to you. What do you do? Do you:

A. call in the army, besiege a city and suspend civil liberties? (*see* Pierre "Just Watch Me" Trudeau)
B. get steamin'-eyed drunk and charge across the floor of the House of Commons and attempt to lambast an Honourable Member with a haymaker to the side of the head? (*see* John A. "I Could Lick You Quicker Than Hell Could Scorch a Feather" Macdonald), or
C. appoint a commissioner to inquire into the problem by interviewing experts, scholars, economists, homemakers, cab drivers, bellboys, convicted felons and anyone else who wants to testify? Do you create by decree a national inquiry, a scrupulous ferreting out of the facts? To report back to the government in, oh, let's say two or three or—what the heck—four years' time?

If you chose C, you win and the nation loses.

Got a problem? Call a commission. There is something deeply Canadian in the very act of deferring judgement. If there is one thing Canadians can agree on, it is that it's best to wait and see. Other nations in the Commonwealth have Royal Commissions as well, but no one has taken to them quite like Canada has.

The catastrophes listed at the beginning of this section actually occurred. And each one was dealt with by a Royal Commission. The Halifax Riots, the Parliament Hill fire of 1916, the Inquiry into Certain Activities of the RCMP ("Certain Activities" being the illegal opening of mail, wiretapping and harassment of citizens; commissions are notoriously euphemistic), the *Ocean Ranger* disaster, and issues ranging from Prohibition to multiculturalism, bi-culturalism, energy, transportation and the status of women—at some point they all came under the authority and vision of a Royal Commission.

In Canada, when the going gets tough, the tough call a commission.

In search of hyperbole, only a Canadian can say: "As Canadian as a Royal Commission."
—*Marshall McLuhan, media guru and master aphorist*

Some Royal Commissions have had a huge impact, for better or for worse. Official bilingualism and free trade, for example, were both spawned by Royal Coms. But those are the exceptions, not the rule. Most Royal Commissions sink without a ripple, and they are used mainly as a way of side-stepping an issue while still maintaining the appearance of Doing Something. (As in, "My God, why doesn't the government Do Something about immigrants/separatism/cold weather/bad breath, etc.")

The name of the game is delay, delay, delay. An incompetent commissioner can stretch out an inquiry for years. A talented one can stretch it out even further. Often, by the time the commission finally presents its voluminous findings, most people have completely forgotten what all the fuss was about. Which is, of course, the whole point. The real problem with Royal Commissions is that they work. Public passion can only run so high for so long, and what is a crisis today is a half-forgotten incident two or three years from now. (Indeed, in Canada a national crisis might well be defined as something that cannot be contained by a Royal Commission.)

Either way, it's the ultimate dog-and-pony show. A travelling bureaucratic burlesque. Leadership by feint. A simple sleight of hand, but one that's pulled on the Canadian public with depressing regularity. Misdirection, of course, is the secret of any good trick. That, and an audience that isn't really paying attention. . .

Canada is fast approaching critical mass in the area of Royal Commissions. There are simply too many commissions running around, squawking away, churning out endless and often hyperbolic recommendations. Keeping track of Royal Commissions is like trying to keep track of serial killers: no one really knows for sure how many are operating out there at any one time.

So how do we solve this problem? The answer is obvious. We need a Royal Commission. That's right: a Royal Commission on Royal Commissions. To be followed, no doubt, by the Royal Commission on the Royal Commission on Royal Commissions, and so on to the vanishing point. And why not? It's the Canadian Way.

CHAPTER 15 SUMMARY: WHAT YOU'VE LEARNED SO FAR

It's inevitable. If you choose Canada as the country to call your own, the day will come when you'll have to explain some rather embarrassing facts of life to your children. So, instead of closing with our usual snappy chapter summary, we thought we would help you—new Canadian that you are—get through this potentially awkward parental moment by presenting the following one-act play, entitled *Fishing with Father,* a powerful new Canadian drama by I. Ferguson.

*   *   *

The banks of a bucolic river somewhere in Canada. A father and his son are fishing. They each cast their lines into the water, then turn to share a moment of happiness and joy in each other's company. It's obvious the fish aren't biting, and it's just as obvious that neither of them really cares.

(The boy momentarily turns away from his father. There is a brief pause, then he turns back with a look of determination on his face.)

Boy: Dad?

Dad: Yes, son?

Boy: Can I ask you something?

Dad: You can ask me anything, son, you know that.

Boy: Okay. It's just that . . .

Dad: What is it, son, what's the matter?

Boy: Dad. Will you tell me about . . . politics?

Dad: Oh. Maybe you should ask your mother—

Boy: She told me to ask you.

Dad: I just think you're a little young to be worrying about politics, son.

Boy: Lately, you know, I've been thinking about voting.

Dad: Oh. My. God.

Boy: Come on, Dad, you've voted. What's it like?

Dad: Now, son, I know you're at that age where you want to be a grown-up and do grown-up things, but trust me, voting isn't that big a deal. You do it by yourself, in a little room, it doesn't last very long, and you always feel sort of dirty and used when it's over.

Boy: Dad? What's a progressive conservative?

Dad: Well, son, that's an oxymoron. Sort of like "responsible government." You see, the Tories used to stand for good fiscal management and strong moral values, but they long ago lost their way.

Boy: How come?

Dad: They got elected. There was this man named Mulroney, and—never mind, you're too young to remember. Power corrupts, son, never forget that. The Tories were proof of this.

Boy: What about the Liberals?

Dad: Absolute power corrupts absolutely.

Boy: And the NDP?

Dad: Having no power corrupts worst of all.

Boy: Well, what about the Canadian Alliance?

Dad: Hmmm. That's a toughie. You let your old dad think for a second.

(The father puts down his fishing rod, and carefully fills and lights his pipe. He puffs thoughtfully on it for a second or two, as his son waits expectantly, but respectfully.)

Dad: Son, do you remember when we rented 2001: A Space Odyssey?

Boy: To mark the millennium.

Dad: That's right. Now, do you remember at the start of the movie, when all the monkeys are jumping around the monolith and they've figured out how to use tools for the first-ever time and they're all excited—

Boy: —yes.

Dad: And do you remember those two monkeys over in the corner who weren't doing anything? They were just eating bugs and playing with their poo? Well, those two monkeys are like the Alliance Party.

Boy: Thanks, Dad. You've really explained everything. I think I *am* a little too young to worry about politics.

Dad: Don't worry, son, you've got nothing but time. Let me just give you one piece of advice. When you're finally old enough to exercise your democratic rights and you step up to that voting booth for the first time—

Boy: Yes, Dad?

Dad: Make sure you take a condom with you, because you're going to get screwed either way.

(The lights fade as the father and son collect their fishing gear and walk away together in a moment that is as magical and eternal as a sunset or the cry of the loon. As always, the best moments in life aren't those that we see or hear, but those we feel.)

16

TWELVE WAYS
TO SAY
"I'M SORRY"

. . . .

How to Be Canadian—

in the Worst Way

*T*HE ESKIMOS of the frozen North have forty words for snow and only one word for sex. College students in sunny southern California have forty words for sex, and none for snow. Each society develops a specialized vocabulary that suits the specific demands of its environment and culture.*

Canadians, who pride themselves on their reputation for politeness, have also evolved linguistically to suit their own particular requirements. Your average Canadian probably could come up with almost as many words for snow as the Inuit, and maybe, oh, say, half as many words for sex as those college kids, but why bother? Canadians may have sex (we certainly have snow), but it doesn't really define our character. Unless you're from Newfoundland.

---

* And yes, we are aware that they are now known as Inuit. And yes, we also know that the forty words for snow is probably an urban legend.

Canadians don't have different words that mean "I'm sorry," but they do have different meanings for the words, as indicated by things like inflection. The use of these two words in combination is very sophisticated and extremely difficult to master, but ultimately worth the sacrifice. Once you learn how to properly say "I'm sorry," you will no longer be trying to *become* Canadian, you will have rewired your brain to such a degree that you will actually *be* Canadian. Now then, as you have no doubt already gathered from the chapter heading, there are twelve variations of "I'm sorry," but be prepared . . . they get more challenging as you go along.

I. The Simple Sorry

The most basic use of "I'm sorry." Can also be shortened to the simpler "Sorry," or amended to the slightly more loquacious "Sorry about that." Used primarily after making unwanted physical contact with another person in a public place.

Eye contact: Not required.

Examples: When bumping into someone as you exit a revolving door; when stepping on someone's foot as you take your seat in a theatre; when backing up into someone in an elevator.

Correct pronunciation: Must be delivered quickly and without inflection. If using either of the longer versions, you must run the words together (i.e., *"I'msorry,"* or *"Sorrybouthat"*).

Sample sentence: "Sorry, I didn't see you."

Actual meaning: "I'm in a hurry and you're in my way."

2. The Essential Sorry

The most common variation of "I'm sorry," and the one you will most often use. Can also be shortened to the simpler "Sorry," but formal usage is preferred. Used primarily when someone makes unwanted physical contact with *you* in a public place.

Eye contact: Optional.

Examples: When someone steps on your foot as you get off an escalator; when someone elbows you on a bus or streetcar; when someone backs into you in a bank lineup.

Correct pronunciation: Must be spoken firmly, with a very slight rising inflection on the first word. If using the shorter version, make sure the "s" in "Sorry" has a slight trace of sibilance.

Sample sentence: "I'm sorry. Isn't this crowd something?"

Actual meaning: "How could you not see me? Are you blind? Or just a jerk?"

3. The Occupational Sorry

This version of "I'm sorry" is to be deployed exclusively within your working environs. Formal usage only. Used primarily when a co-worker desires your undivided attention.

Eye contact: Fleeting.

Examples: When the phone in your office rings in the middle of an informal meeting; when a co-worker asks you a question five minutes before quitting time; when the same co-worker asks if you'd like to look at pictures from their vacation in Mexico.

Correct pronunciation: Falling inflection, slight emphasis on the "I'm." (A faint tone of regret is also recommended.)

Sample sentence: "I'm sorry, I really have to take this call."

Actual meaning: "I would really rather talk to an aluminum siding salesman than spend another moment listening to you."

4. The Subservient Sorry

This "I'm sorry" is also exclusive to your place of work. Again, only the formal usage is allowed. This time, however, it is used when dealing with a client or customer.

Eye contact: Evasive.

Examples: When a client asks you for contract concessions; when a customer asks you for help finding the right size; when a patron asks for more coffee.

Correct pronunciation: A rising inflection with a slight questioning tone at the end.

Sample sentence: "I'm sorry? Is there something wrong with the veal?"

Actual meaning: "I would like to stab you through the eye with this olive fork."

5. The Aristocratic Sorry

This "I'm sorry" is used mainly in social situations when you are the customer or client. Formal usage is encouraged and, for greater effect, you can insert the word "very" in between the "I'm" and the "sorry." Used mainly when you require some sort of service.

Eye contact: Compulsory.

Examples: When you want a simple contract concession

from your supplier; when you just need a little bit of help finding the right outfit; when you would like another cup of coffee.

Correct pronunciation: Flat inflection. Equal emphasis on both words. Slight pause between words, or, if you are adding the linguistic flourish of the "very," a slight pause before it, and a slightly longer pause after it.

Sample sentence: "I'm . . . very . . . sorry, but this isn't the entree I ordered."

Actual meaning: "Don't you know who I am? I've had people killed for less!"

6. The Demonstrative Sorry

This "I'm sorry" works best when used with a partner or loved one. Formal usage is generally appropriate, and this time you can add the word "very" as many times as you want. Used when you've either done something you *weren't* supposed to do, or not done something you *were* supposed to do.

Eye contact: Beseechingly.

Examples: When you've arrived somewhere too early; when you've arrived somewhere too late; when you have forgotten a significant date.

Correct pronunciation: Rising inflection building to near-hysteria. If possible, string the words together into one continuous verbal outpouring of emotion.

Sample sentence: "I'm veryveryveryvery sorry. Really. You have no idea how sorry I am."

Actual meaning: "Why are you so angry? Was it something I said?" (Males only: He knew he was a dead man, but he must now race against time to find out why.)

"Was it something I *should* have said?" (Females only: "What is it that I'm supposed to have done this time? I am really getting tired of your moods.")

7. The Libidinous Sorry

This "I'm sorry" usually follows in direct chronological order from the above. Formal usage only, and don't try to get fancy with this. Used with partner or loved one in private quarters.

Eye contact: Constant.

Examples: When riding home in a taxi with loved one or partner after a fight at a party; walking home with loved one or partner after a disagreement over movie choice at the video store; getting into bed with partner or loved one after not speaking to each other all day.

Correct pronunciation: Equal emphasis on both words, slight rising inflection on "sorry."

Sample sentence: "I'm sorry. I was wrong. Please forgive me."

Actual meaning: "You're wrong, I'm right, but I'm tired of fighting and I hope this shift in tactics will lead to some foolin' around."

8. The Ostentatious Sorry

This "I'm sorry" can be used in a wide range of situations and conversations. For maximum effect, you should employ the shorter "Sorry" version. Used chiefly as a reactive tool in establishing status.

Eye contact: Condescendingly.

Examples: When someone asks if you're planning to sign

up for the bonspiel; when someone tries to tell you about a fascinating television program they watched the night before; when someone uses a word you don't understand.

Correct pronunciation: Slight rising inflection. Quizzical tonality.

Sample sentence: ". . . sorry?"

Actual meaning: "I'm pretending that I didn't hear and/or didn't understand your last statement, but we both know that what you just said proves how stupid and uncultured you are. You are truly beneath contempt. Now, breathe in the glory that is me. Bow down before me. I am your superior in this and all things that truly matter."

9. The Mythical Sorry

This "I'm sorry" is used to support a personal recollection or anecdote. Any variation or usage could potentially work, although the simplest, most straightforward version will also be the most effective. Can be used when talking to a group of people or an individual friend or acquaintance.

Eye contact: Penetrating.

Examples: When you are describing a recent bout of bad service; when you are talking about a fight you just had with your boss; when you are telling someone about a recent minor traffic accident.

Correct pronunciation: Rising inflection, huge emphasis on the first syllable of "Sorry." You can also snap your fingers dismissively for further dramatic effect.

Sample sentence: "So I looked him in the eye and I said to him, 'Look, I'm sorry, but this is unacceptable.'"

Actual meaning: "I didn't say anything. I'm a fraud. I backed down. I chickened out, and my greatest fear is that you will figure out what a coward I am. Please oh please, just put me out of my misery. Sob."

10. The Unrepentant Sorry

This extremely sophisticated variation of "I'm sorry" is used to fend off any justified criticism you might encounter. Formal usage works best, although politicians are starting to experiment with the diminutive version with great success.

Eye contact: If necessary, but not necessarily eye contact.

Examples: When you say something stupid, and then you pretend you never said it, but then a reporter had their tape recorder running and now you're busted, and everyone is asking you to clarify your statements; when you have to go on television and explain why you used taxpayers' money to cover your legal fees; when you park too close to another car and open your door so hard that you put a dent in the other car and the owner of that car happens to be standing right there and he says, "Do you know that you just put a dent in my car?"

Correct pronunciation: Downward inflection, slight breath between the "I'm" and the "sorry," can be supported by slight shrug of shoulders.

Sample sentence: "I'm, um, sorry. . ."

Actual meaning: "I'm not sorry for what I did, I'm just sorry I got caught."

11. The Sympathetic Sorry

This variation of "I'm sorry" can only be properly performed if you have a good understanding of what the Germans mean by *schadenfreude*. It is always used with a modifying "so" in the middle. And always at times of great pain and loss. For someone else.

Eye contact: Constantly.

Examples: When a co-worker tells you he's just been fired; when an old flame arrives at your door at two o'clock in the morning crying her eyes out; when a neighbour tells you he has just discovered he is going to be audited.

Correct pronunciation: Rising inflection on the first word, falling inflection on the second word, a flat inflection on the last word.

Sample sentence: "I'm . . . *so* . . . sorry."

Actual meaning: "I'm so happy that this is happening to you and not me. I revel in your downfall!"

12. The Authentic Sorry

The least used of all of our dozen variations. What can we say? We didn't spend a lot of time researching this one. Sorry about that.

Eye contact: Hard to say. Sorry.

Examples: Sorry, but we can't really come up with any examples . . .

Correct pronunciation: Who the hell knows? Oh, jeez. Sorry about the profanity.

Sample sentence: Sample sentence. Ooh. That's a tough one. Can't think of any. Sorry.

Actual meaning: Some sort of expression of regret? Sorry. Don't really know.

And there you have it. Your own personal 12-step program to mastering the Canadian art of saying "I'm sorry." Canadians use that expression the way cab drivers use car horns, for just about any situation that comes along.

Canadians say "sorry" an awful lot. But they rarely apologize.

17

YOU MAY ALREADY BE A CANADIAN!

. . . .

*Take the Quiz
and Find Out*

1. If you hear the name "Elvis" and immediately think of figure skating, give yourself 1 point.

2. If you hear the name "Marilyn" and immediately think of swimming Lake Ontario: 5 points.

3. If you hear the name "Preston" and immediately think of Lee "pressed-on" nails: subtract 6 points.

4. If you thought *Degrassi Junior High* was a gripping true-life docu-drama: 2 points.

5. If you have a "Bring Back Degrassi" website: subtract 2 points.

6. But if it's an "ironic" website, that's okay. Add 3 points.

7. If you think your friends sitting around your basement eating Doritos would make an excellent episode of *The Lofters*: minus 2 points.

8. If you think Snow Job is way cooler than Mardi Gras: add 1 point.

9. If you have ever, ever, *ever* appeared on *Speaker's Corner* for any reason whatsoever, give yourself a slap in the face. From all of us.

10. Unless you got your own TV series out of it (like the Devil's Advocates). In that case, add 1 point.

11. If you ever went to a rave onboard a chartered yellow schoolbus: deduct 1 point.

12. If you wear an "Anarchy Now!" T-shirt, but get mad when guests come over and don't use the coasters: 1 point.

13. If you think the cover of Naomi Klein's book *No Logo* would make an excellent logo: 2 points.

14. If you own a "Canadian Girls Kick Ass" T-shirt: 1 point.

15. Even though you, yourself, would never kick ass: 2 points.

16. If you were at the Quebec City "Clash of the Summits," add 10 points.

17. If you were there selling hot dogs, deduct 20 points.

18. If they were special "No Logo Anarchy Now!" hot dogs, your credentials are restored. Give yourself a hand.

19. If you still don't know what the capital of New Brunswick is, give yourself 10 points.

20. If you have been to Niagara Falls: 1 point.

21. In a barrel: 100 points.

22. If you've ever had a Nanaimo bar. In a bar. In Nanaimo: give yourself 2 points.

23. If you can ask the operator to look up a number in Dildo, Newfoundland, without feeling any embarrassment, give yourself 1 point.

24. If you can stop for gas in Climax, Saskatchewan, and not make any wisecracks: 3 points.

25. If you can say "Regina" without giggling, give yourself 12 points.

26. If you've ever posed for a picture beside a Large Object Next to a Highway, give yourself 1 point.

27. If you've ever posed for a picture beside a provincial boundary sign, give yourself 3 points.

28. If you've ever posed for a picture with professional curler Hec Gervais, give yourself five hundred million points.

29. If you mistakenly thought he was the statue of Jumbo the Elephant in St. Thomas, Ontario, deduct 9 points.

30. If you have ever curled, give yourself 1 point.

31. If you were the skip, give yourself 2 points.

32. If you can't remember if you curled or not, because of how drunk you were: 50 points.

33. If you remember where you were when the Jays won the World Series: 1 point.

34. If you remember where you were the day Ben got caught: 1 point.

35. If you remember where you were the day Wayne was traded: 1 point.

36. If you didn't need last names on those to know who we were talking about: 3 points.

37. If you remember where you were when Baltimore won the Grey Cup: deduct 12 points.

38. If you remember (vividly) what you were doing the day Bob Homme died: 2 points.

39. If you knew that Bob Homme was the Friendly Giant: 6 points.

40. If you cried, even though you hadn't watched his show since you were six years old: 12 points.

41. If you remember where you were the day Trudeau died: 1 point.

42. If you remember where you were the day Stan Rogers died: 2 points.

43. If you know almost all the words to "Barrett's Privateers" but you don't know the words to the national anthem: 10 points.

44. If you still know all the words to the Molson "I am Canadian" rant: minus 20 points.

45. If you're glad they finally drove that schtick into the ground: 1 point.

46. (Bonus question for Boomers) If you think the Canadian gull-winged Bricklin sports car was actually kind of cool: 1 point.

47. Even though you drive a Dodge Neon: 1 point.

48. Which you are proud to own, since most of it was manufactured in Ontario: 10 points.

49. If you understand the Auto Pact: 5 points.

50. No, you don't.: minus 6 points.

51. If you understand the offside rule in hockey: 10 points.

52. (Really? Can you explain it to us? Because we've never figured the damn thing out.)

53. If you don't understand the economy: 1 point.

54. But you invest anyway: subtract 3 points.

55. Because you trust your broker: subtract an additional 8 points, plus most of your life savings.

56. If you complain about rush hour: 5 points.

57. Even though you live in Victoria: 10 points.

58. And actually walk to work. 15 points.

59. If you have never made love in a canoe: 1 point.

60. If you wouldn't even know how to begin to do that: 3 points.

61. In fact, you think it's kind of a stupid and dangerous idea: 6 points.

62. I mean, really, the government should put up a warning label about that sort of thing, right? 1 point.

63. And it's not the least bit erotic: 9 points.

64. I mean, where would you put your feet? 12 points.

65. And does wearing water wings constitute "safe sex"? 2 points.

66. If you have actually paddled a canoe: 1 point.

67. If it was at summer camp: 3 points.

68. In the Adirondacks: deduct 20 points.

69. If you think Don McKellar is a better director than Atom Egoyan: 1 point.

70. But neither of them could hold a candle to Norman Jewison: 2 points.

71. Or Ivan Reitman: deduct 37 points. (What, are you nuts or something?)

72. If you think Jim Carrey is funnier than Mike Myers: 1 point.

73. But both of them are funnier than Tom Green: 2 points.

74. If you have no idea who Tom Green is: deduct 3 points, and congratulations on your new position as head of talent development at the CBC.

75. If, whenever you think about the complicated and sometimes difficult relationship you had with your father, you wonder if the problems you had relating to each other had to do with the fact that you were constantly comparing him to the famous, fictional father figures that Canadian actors seem to specialize in: 1 point.

76. Like Lorne Greene in *Bonanza*: 1 point.

77. Or Christopher Plummer in *The Sound of Music*: 2 points.

78. Or Lorne Greene in *Battlestar Galactica*: 3 points.

79. Which you thought was a better show than *Lost in Space*: 1 point.

80. If you think *Space 1999,* a British science fiction series that featured Canadian actor Barry Morse for the first season, was superior to *The Starlost,* a Canadian science fiction series that starred Keir Dullea and lasted for one season: 1 point.

81. If you haven't seen either of those shows, but you do remember Keir Dullea from his performance in that classic Canadian movie *Leopard in the Snow*: 50 points.

82. Which, you may recall, was the worst film ever made: 1 point.

83. And which, we just found out, *is* available on video: 10 points.

84. Not that we've ever been able to find it: minus 5 points.

85. If you refuse to believe William Shatner wears a hairpiece: 1 point.

86. If you refuse to believe Rich Little wears a hairpiece: 2 points.

87. If you refuse to believe Jeffrey Simpson wears a hairpiece: What, are you blind? Deduct 7 points.

88. If you think Ken Kostick *does* wear a hairpiece: 5 points.

89. If you have been to a real sugar shack and eaten real 100% maple syrup fresh from the tree: 10 points.

90. If it was in Maine: deduct 30 points.

91. But you secretly prefer the taste of Aunt Jemima: add 2 points.

92. If this makes you feel guilty: 6 points.

93. If you have ever eaten a beaver tail: 3 points.

94. Not a sugared pastry from Ottawa, but an actual beaver's tail: 10 points.

95. If you recently caught a glimpse of the Northern Lights: 1 point.

96. If you immediately and inexplicably remembered some lines from a Robert Service poem: 3 points.

97. Which freaked you out, since you're pretty sure that you've never actually read any Robert Service: 6 points.

98. If you began to ponder the idea of the collective unconscious: 12 points.

99. If you think Marshall McLuhan came up with that theory: 1 point.

100. Then you remember he didn't: deduct 3 points.

101. If you start to think about other stuff you might know that you didn't think you knew—and it turns out you can remember huge chunks of W.O. Mitchell: 1 point.

102. Well, hell, you probably studied him in school: 2 points.

103. If you can quote passages from books by Robertson Davies, Hugh Garner or Margaret Laurence: deduct 10 points. What are you, some kind of freak?

104. If you hop into your new PT Cruiser—built in Detroit, though the seat covers are made right here—and stop at a Starbucks for a latte, and then pick up the latest issue of *People* from your corner 7-Eleven, rent *American President, American Beauty* and *American History* at your local Blockbuster, go home and watch them on your cozy Ikea Sklönjebeldt sofa, and, without any irony at all, feel sort of proud to be Canadian: 1 point.

105. If this also makes you feel guilty: 6 points.

106. But you get over it: 9 points.

107. Because you bought this book: 50 points.

RATING YOUR SCORE

90 points or more: Wow, you're either incredibly knowledgeable or you cheated. Either way, you're scaring us.

Between 60 and 90 points: You teach Canadian history at a community college or university and you read this book in the mistaken belief it might help you prepare a class plan. It won't. Sorry.

Between 30 and 60 points: Right in the middle. Good for you. You're not only a Canadian, you're confused and conflicted about what that even means. Welcome to the club.

Between 10 and 30 points: Technically, you may be a Canadian, but only in the way that someone like Ezra Levant is Canadian. Good luck with your green card application; we're not going to miss you.

Less than 10 points: Not only are you NOT Canadian, you didn't even flip through the rest of this book. You guessed at the answers. Heck, you probably found this book in the seat pocket of a transatlantic flight. *Tch.*

Zero points: So, you couldn't even be bothered to do the damn quiz. Too much effort, eh? You just skipped to the end. Talk about slack. Talk about lazy. Talk about Canadian! Congratulations. You are now one of us.

ACKNOWLEDGEMENTS

*P*ARTS OF this book first appeared in a slightly different form in the *Ottawa Citizen* as part of a series entitled "Canada 101," and Will would like to thank Sue Allan and Mike Gillespie at the *Citizen*. Thanks also to Columpa C. Bobb, who saved the day by loaning Ian the use of her laptop when he was in Winnipeg.

WILL FERGUSON (the one with the beard) is the author of several national best-sellers, including *Bastards & Bone-heads, Canadian History for Dummies* and the tongue-in-cheek survey *Why I Hate Canadians.* He is also the author of a bittersweet memoir about coming of age in Canada in the 1980s, entitled *I Was a Teenage Katima-victim!* His debut novel, *Generica,* was hailed by the *Globe and Mail* as "an uncompromising and brilliant satire."

IAN FERGUSON (the one without the beard) is an award-winning playwright—*Elephant Shoes, Uncle Joe Again, The Daughters of Judy LaMarsh* and *Naming the Animals,* among others—and theatrical director. He is the creator of the live improvised soap operas *Die-Nasty* and *Sin City* and is the executive producer of the *Sin City* television series.